2837
4978

CARSON CITY LIBRARY

A Homesteader's Portfolio

Alice Day Pratt

Introduction by Molly Gloss

Oregon State University Press
Corvallis, Oregon

The paper in this book meets the guidelines for permanence and durability of the Committee on Production Guidelines for Book Longevity of the Council on Library Resources and the minimum requirements of the American National Standard for Permanence of Paper for Printed Library Materials Z39.48-1984.

Library of Congress Cataloging-in-Publication Data

Pratt, Alice Day.
A homesteader's portfolio / Alice Day Pratt ; introduction by Molly Gloss.
p. cm. -- (Northwest reprints)
Originally published: New York : Macmillan, 1922.
Includes bibliographical references.
ISBN 0-87071-516-X. — ISBN 0-87071-517-8 (pbk. alk. paper)
1. Pratt, Alice Day. 2. Women pioneers--Oregon--Biography. 3. Pioneers--Oregon--Biography. 4. Farm life--Oregon. 5. Agriculture--Oregon. 6. Oregon--Biography. I. Title. II. Series.
F881.P93P73 1993
979.5'04'092--dc20
[B] 93-24254
CIP

Introduction © 1993 Molly Gloss
All rights reserved
Printed in the United States of America

PREFACE

but there were things
That covered what a man was, and set him apart
From others, things by which others knew him. The place
Where he lived, the horse he rode, his relatives, his wife,
His voice, complexion, beard, politics, religion or lack of it,
And so on. With time, these things fall away
Or dwindle into shadows: river sand blowing away
From some long-buried old structure of bleached boards
That appears a vague shadow through the sand-haze,
and then stands clear,
Naked, angular, itself.
from "Trial and Error," H.L. Davis

People new to a region are especially interested in what things might set them apart from others. In works by Northwest writers, we get to know about the place where we live, about each other, about our history and culture, and about our flora and fauna. And with time, some things about ourselves start to come into focus out of the shadows of our history.

To give readers an opportunity to look into the place where Northwesterners live, the Oregon State University Press is making available again many books that are out of print. The Northwest Reprints Series will reissue a range of books, both fiction and nonfiction. Books will be selected for different reasons: some for their literary merit, some for their historical significance, some for provocative concerns, and some for these and other reasons together. Foremost, however, will be the book's potential to interest a range of readers who are curious about the region's voice and complexion. The Northwest Reprints Series will make works of well-known and lesser-known writers available for all.

RJF

Alice Day Pratt and the Homestead Dream

In 1910 Alice Day Pratt was 38 years old, in her own words an "old maid" school teacher, and labor troubles had just released her from a three-year stint teaching in Arkansas coal camps. She had come to a hinge point in her life. "I realized that I was *tired*—tired both *by* and *of* my work," she would write more than forty years later in her self-published memoir *Three Frontiers.* After fifteen years of teaching, "closely hedged about by organization, boards, principals, superintendents, wise and otherwise parental interference," she took stock of her life and formed what must have seemed to her friends and colleagues a singular and reckless intent. She accepted a summer teaching position to earn the price of a ticket West—salaries in the South had been low, she'd saved nothing; and teaching took on a different aspect when she saw it as a bridge to a new life. She sent to the Department of the Interior for maps of unappropriated lands available for homestead, and to the Department of Agriculture for literature on the best uses to which such lands could be put. When she had narrowed her search to Oregon, she began to read the history and geography—"everything"—about the region. She then wrote to the Oregon State Superintendent of Schools. Swiftly, she had the offer of a teaching position in Athena, then and now a small community in the wheat country northeast of Pendleton. And in September of 1911, she and her dog boarded a train bound for Oregon.

It was the first step in her strategy for "building a farm"—but not the first time Alice Day Pratt had turned her face toward a frontier.[1]

*

When William McLain Pratt and Sophie Rand had married in 1869 they had made a home in Meriden, Connecticut, with William's aged father, Julius. Within months of their marriage, Julius was dead and William had inherited his portion of his father's estate. He took this as a salutary sign. He had been wounded at the Battle of Antietam, his health never wholly recovered, and he had been advised to seek the drier climate of the West—advice that fell in with his inclinations. "He had all the adventurousness of his pioneer ancestors," his daughter later would write, for William's namesake had been among the founders of Connecticut. Sophie Rand didn't share her husband's adventurousness, but was, as Alice Pratt described her, "one of those for whom decisions are made." In the fall of 1870, William moved his wife and infant daughter, Sophie Caroline, to Blue Earth County, Minnesota, where they settled into a house on a wooded bluff above Mankato, the county seat, with grand views north and south along the Minnesota River valley. Their second daughter, Alice, was born there in 1872.[2]

---

1. All biographical information concerning Alice Pratt's childhood in Minnesota and Dakota Territory derives from her memoir, *Three Frontiers.*

2. It's a difficult problem: how to refer to Alice Pratt in a way that is both respectful and graceful. Repeated usage of her full name is cumbersome, to say the least, and her last name used alone—perhaps just

The playground of Alice's childhood was the land this house sat upon—"a fenced-off tract of native forest with its accompanying inhabitants." Her lifelong affinity for animals had its roots here. On a fishing expedition early in her childhood—"one of the first pictures in my memory"—Alice recalled helping her father catch small frogs and put them in a box in the end of the boat. "I thought they were to be 'pets.' When I saw my father make use of them for bait I was very sick. When the fish lay gasping and flopping in the boat they were nearly as bad. There was a cloud over my day. . . . We were to take this trip to the lake again, in the autumn, and I was to see my father bring in flocks of quail and loads of ducks. I stroked their beautiful soft feathers and admired their iridescent colors, but their poor dead eyes, the blood dripping from their beaks! Why was my father so happy to have done this?" (*Frontiers*, pp. 2-3).

Here, also, the foundations were laid for her attitudes of conservation and stewardship of the land. Flocks of passenger pigeons darkened the sky in migrating season, above a prairie exuberant with flying squirrels and sand-hill cranes, all destined for extinction at the hands of her neighbors. "The beauty of the prairies and the destruction of prairie life! These go together in my memory as they go together in our history" (*Frontiers*, p.3).

---

because of its inherent unmelodiousness—seems brusque and surly. Other writers would doubtless reach other conclusions, but after weeks of living very nearly inside Alice's life, I find I am most comfortable referring to her as I would a friend—with grace and respect—by her given name.

Alice's father had invested his entire inheritance, as well as money entrusted for investment by his wife's relatives, in a Mankato lumbering business; after three consecutive years of a destructive grasshopper scourge, farmers began to lose their farms to mortgagees, and William's business, dependent on farmers' prosperity, also began to fail. The Black Hills had just been opened to settlement and he turned in that direction, not with the intent of prospecting for gold but hopeful that rapid settlement of the Dakotas would open possibilities for lumbermen. Alice stood with her mother and sister, watching him away in a wagon weighted with mill machinery.

It would be years before the family was reunited—William came and went but would not consider moving his family into country so rough as the Black Hills were in those days. "I think our adventurous father never really appreciated the effect of this move on our young mother," Alice wrote. "He was, to the end of his life, unswervingly devoted to her—but he was sustained in their separation by the excitement of the adventure, the buoyant hope of success, and the firm belief that he would bring prosperity to her again, while she had only the waiting and the loneliness. There was sorrow too, which she had to bear alone. For in 1882, death struck twice in the space of a few months—first my older sister [Sophie Caroline], who was in her twelfth year, and then a baby sister, hardly more than a year old" (*Frontiers*, pp.13-14).

Eventually William claimed a homestead in Little Elk Canyon, twenty-five miles from his business in Deadwood, and after a summer visit in 1883, Alice and her mother came permanently to the canyon in 1886. The site was remote—for many years it was accessible only by horseback—and positioned as a kind of gateway to perhaps a thousand acres of unsurveyed, untouched timber-land—"one of the most beautiful of natural sanctuaries."

For nearly fifteen years, they lived in a five-room cabin two miles from stores, post office, neighbors. Two more children were born into the family in 1888 and 1891. Alice's grandfather, Sophie's widowed father, also joined the house-hold, but with Grandfather Rand suffering from rheumatism and asthma, and William often away tending to his lumber business in Deadwood, much of the heavy work fell to Alice. Water was carried in pails up a steep slope from the spring or the creek, and foodstuffs not grown in the garden had to be brought by horseback, later by wagon, from the small store two miles off, or from Rapid City, fifteen miles away. The horses were let out to range the canyon and had to be brought in when they were needed. In winter, trips to the store and post office would meet the bitter north wind that blew down the trough of the Red Valley. "I once, having had my scarf blown off, froze my ears so hard that I took them for the brim of my hat and struggled to push them up into place. When I reached home and was made painfully aware of the situation, I envisioned having my ears drop off like the combs of unfortunate roosters I had seen" (*Frontiers*, p.37).

Yet Alice remembered it as an idyllic time. "We were always warm in the house and no fears beset us. Life was so simple that not much could happen to it." They were always busy in the daylight hours, and in the winter evenings they had a custom of reading around the table from a "little library" and a wide array of periodicals "of which we had always had the best, as a necessity of life"—*The Atlantic Monthly, Harper's, The Century, Scribner's, St. Nicholas, The Youth's Companion.*

On horseback with her friend Mamie Gardner, Alice ranged the valleys and neighboring canyons, the nearby plains. It wasn't uncommon for the two girls to cover forty miles horseback in a day's excursion—riding out, lunching on the buffalo grass carpet where they would lie down "exchanging views" before riding home again slowly by another route. Home schooled, Alice became interested in botany, and made a vast if amateurish collection of Black Hills flora. It was a solitary pursuit that she felt may have increased her "separateness." "The thrill of my adolescence became the discovery of a new plant, the nest of a hitherto unknown bird, the meeting with a wild creature. . . . In these excursions and in the lone study of my books, I spent the hours that I would naturally have spent with my own kind—for good or ill?" (*Frontiers*, p. 49).

At the end of 1900, William Pratt sold the Little Elk Canyon property and moved his family to the Blue Ridge country of North Carolina, where he transferred his lumber interests. Alice had already been away from home studying and teaching for several years, but she followed her family to the region and went on teaching, mostly in North Carolina, until her long-latent, long-suppressed desire to "take [my] portion of the earth's crust" put her on a train to Oregon.

In Athena she immediately came up against the local school board, and almost as soon as she had accepted her position there she had submitted her resignation, taking a moral stand in support of a young, unjustly treated teacher. Within a month she had the offer of another position at a newly formed school on the Stanfield Irrigation Project, thirty-five miles to the west. A planned community of irrigated homesteads carved out of what had been a vast sheep ranch, Stanfield was for the most part occupied by affluent farmers who had come here after successfully homesteading elsewhere.

A farm in Stanfield was out of the question for someone of Alice's vanishingly small means, and accordingly she hired a "locator" to scout out prospective properties in the public domain. In November she filed on 160 acres at the foot of Friar Butte, southeast of Prineville near the tiny community of Post, and the following spring gave up her position at Stanfield and moved onto the land she had named "Broadview." It is the story of this homestead, the events of the first five years "proving up" on the land, that is told in *A Homesteader's Portfolio.*

In the fall of 1916—as soon as her five-year residency requirement had been met—Alice went East to spend time with her family. Land laws did not require a homesteader to live on the claim after proving up, and she was anxious to get her finances on a better footing, so for two years she lived and worked in the East, returning to Broadview in the summer of 1918. Soon afterward she took a teaching post at the Conant Basin school, in the Maury Mountains ten miles west of Broadview.[3] She spent two winters at Conant, bringing her band of Jersey cows, seven horses, her flock of White Leghorn chickens, a dog and several cats with her "over the rimrock," and settling first into a vacant ranch close to the schoolhouse, then occupying a house near the Crooked River, three miles from the schoolhouse.[4]

Both years in the Basin, her routine included a weekly trip to Friar Butte. "On Saturdays I baked and brewed and churned and washed for the week to come. On Sundays I made a trip to the homestead, ten miles distant. I usually made this a round trip by descending over the Rim and return-

---

3. Biographical information on Alice's life in these later homesteading years, 1918-1930, has been gathered from her unpublished manuscript, *Teacher's Trek,* from Brooks Ragen's unpublished manuscript "Alice Day Pratt in Oregon," and from my interviews with the Pratt family. "Dinner in the Basin," Chapter XIV of A *Homesteader's Portfolio,* describes a social visit over the rimrock to Conant Basin; it is very likely that her long-standing friendships in the area led to her teaching post at the Conant school.

4. In *Teacher's Trek,* Pratt wrote: ". . . three miles, across bleak fields, in sunshine and storm, in heat and cold, took more or less out of the teacher. I made the journey most often on foot, because I could slip through the intervening fences, which necessitated a weary around for a horse" (Chapter 7, p.9). Alice was

ing by the river ford—an almost all day trip on a winter's day" (*Trek*, chapt. 7, p.6). It was probably during her winters in Conant Basin that she began work on the book that would be *A Homesteader's Portfolio*, fleshing it out from the personal journal she had kept throughout her five years proving up at Broadview.

Though the dates are uncertain, Alice later took a teaching position at the Maury school, twenty miles east of Post, and apparently spent some winters in Western Oregon. In the winter of 1927, for instance, she lived in Wheeler on the Oregon coast and took a correspondence course in short story writing.[5] And during this time, too, she was probably at work on her only novel, *Sagebrush Fires*, which mirrored much of her own experience as a woman homesteader.[6]

---

known throughout the Post area for her inclination to walk great distances in all manner of weather. See Clarine Silver, "The Old Maid of Friar Butte," *Eugene Register Guard* (April 23, 1972), and Beverly Wolverton, *A Hundred and Sixty Acres in the Sage: Homestead History of the Immediate Post Area* (Post, Oregon: Beverly Wolverton, 1984).

5. Brooks Ragen, "Alice Day Pratt in Oregon" (unpublished ms, 1976), pp.28-29. In *Animals of a Sagebrush Ranch,* Alice gives a poignant account of "Peggy" and her dog, having lost the trail on a day hike between Wheeler and Cannon Beach, wandering lost in the Coast Range for four rainy nights and days—an ordeal that Alice's family recalls as true.

6. *Sagebrush Fires I* and *II* comprise a two-part novel set in the Maury Mountains in the 1910s and 20s. As cited by Brooks Ragen, the heroine of *Sagebrush Fires*

By the late 1920s, from a single pregnant cow, she had built a herd of some one hundred Jerseys. But she was often in precarious financial straits. In 1929 "drought was upon us by the first of June. For six months, dry or drying pasture was inevitable even on many theoretically irrigated fields. Hay prices soared 100 percent and more. Cream prices, by some strange economic law, dropped 50 percent" ("Jerseys," p. 52). In the fall she was driven to place a dangerously large loan on her dairy herd. The following autumn, with the Oregon dairy business reeling from the recent business crash, butterfat dropping to "teen cents a pound" and eggs to twenty cents, she was forced to sell her Jerseys for the amount of the loan. And at the close of the year, "not only penniless but in debt," Alice left Broadview "which I had so dearly loved for eighteen years" and moved to Niagara Falls to take up housekeeping with her mother and younger sister Marjorie. She held on to the ranch for some twenty years more, but never returned to Oregon. The homestead was finally sold in 1950, to the neighbor into whose care she had, years earlier, given over her horses and chickens.[7]

---

is a woman, Barbara Wescott, who is homesteading a small ranch. Unmarried until near the end of the book, she spends her non-working hours reading science and "the great novels." The man she ultimately marries, John Farnham, is a wealthy Western artist. Their home is "famed as a centre [sic] of free discussion. The only idea that does not receive hospitality there is the idea that the last word of wisdom has been pronounced on any subject" (Part II, p.80).

7. Silver, p.11.

In the first year after leaving Broadview, Alice may have devoted herself to writing.[8] In 1931 two essays appeared in *The Atlantic Monthly,* as well as a children's book of stories, *Animals of a Sagebrush Ranch*; a third essay appeared in *The Atlantic* in 1932. At least one of her unpublished manuscripts also dates from this time. Over the next twenty-odd years she went on writing, as well as teaching occasionally—including a year on remote and primitive Smith Island in Chesapeake Bay—but her publishing success after 1932 was only marginal. In 1941 a second children's book, *Animal Babies,* was released by Beacon Press, an imprint of the Episcopal Church. And in 1955 Alice's brother, Julius W. Pratt,[9] financed a private printing of *Three Frontiers,* which in addition to recounting her Oregon homesteading experience included memories of her childhood in Minnesota and Dakota. But much of her work remains unpublished, including her novel, *Sagebrush Fires,* several short stories that relate in some way to her Oregon years, and *Teacher's Trek,* a memoir of her teaching life which includes the years spent in central Oregon.

In 1937, Alice, together with her sister and mother, moved to a New York City apartment. "I

8. Biographical information regarding Alice Pratt's later life has been gathered from my interviews with the Pratt family, from Clarine Silver, "The Old Maid of Friar Butte," and from Brooks Ragen, "Alice Day Pratt in Oregon."

9. Alice's brother, whom she referred to affectionately as "J.W.," was an internationally recognized historian in the field of American diplomatic history.

am sitting this morning at the window of my room in a New York City apartment house," she wrote in *Teacher's Trek*. "My view is limited up and down, from side to side, by hard stone walls. If I thrust my head far out of the window, I may see a little patch of blue sky above and a stone court below. . . . My mind goes back to a high, sky-topped, brilliant and wind-swept region, mountains rising on the south, cliffs falling away to the river on the north, snow-capped mountains towering on the far horozon [sic] for those who ride the high trails" (Chapter 7, p.4). Alice's passion for animals and for wild landscapes continued unabated. During a teaching stint in the Finger Lakes district of New York State, she bought a used bread-delivery truck without an engine, set it on blocks and lived in it, and when the Finger Lakes position ended she had the bread truck-cum-cabin moved to Old Forge, New York, in the Adirondack Mountains. For many years Alice used this as her summer retreat, living in the company of her dog and cat, carrying water in pails from the spring a quarter of a mile away, and trudging the mile and a half to town for her groceries, just as she'd done at Broadview, and in her childhood at Little Elk Canyon.

In the last years of her life a crippling arthritis confined her to a small room above the East River on 116th street. Her mother had died in 1940, and Marjorie, who had held various teaching positions in and near New York, finally gave up teaching and dedicated several years to caring for her sister. Though Alice's eyesight deteriorated, she remained able to use the typewriter, and she continued to write letters, to listen to the news, and to welcome friends, who obligingly read to her from a wide, "necessary" array of newspapers and magazines. When she died in 1963 Alice was 91, her intellect and her spirit emphatically undiminished at the end of a long, venturesome life.

*

Roused to seek "the glory and the dream," Alice was one among tens of thousands of people who took up homesteads in the arid West in the early twentieth century. More than a handful in that throng—perhaps as many as 18 percent—were like Alice, single women.[10]

In *A Homesteader's Portfolio,* single women homesteaders are in conspicuous evidence. The "Dakota girl of Bohemian parentage," who befriends Alice in her stay at Stanfield, had bought a relinquishment near her brother's homestead on the Hermiston Project.[11] Alice's Broadview neigh-

---

10. Of the several studies of homestead entries made by women, the most frequently cited is the Wyoming and Colorado sampling reported by Sheryll and Gene Patterson-Black, which originally appeared in *Frontiers: A Journal of Women Studies* I (Summer 1976), but which I encountered in slightly different form in *Western Women in History and Literature* (Crawford, Nebraska: Cottonwood Press, 1978). The Patterson-Blacks report an average of 11.9 percent of homestead entrants were women in samples taken from land records in Lamar, Colorado, and Douglas, Wyoming. In sample years, percentages varied from 4.8 percent in Douglas in 1891 to 18.2 percent in Lamar in 1907. Other writers have estimated as much as one-third of Western lands may have been held by women.

11. Unsuccessful homesteaders "relinquished" their

bor, Mary Porter, was "a homestead spinster like myself." The "Nash girls," children of early settlers, lived with their brothers on the family stock ranch, but each had filed a homestead claim, and joined in operating the ranch as a family unit.[12] Mrs. Dunham is mentioned as "a widow and newcomer . . . living in a tent," though Alice wryly observes that "the cattle country has its own way of looking after widowhood. It eliminates the condition."

Alice and her neighbors represent the broad range of women drawn westward by the same mythos that drew men: the promise of free land, and the freedom to "live my own life in my own

---

claims to the government. But people who gave up their claims before gaining title to the land often tried to recoup the investments they had already made by selling their relinquishments rather than turning them back to the public domain. Buyers were given credit for the time that had already been spent on the claims, and took over responsibility for fulfilling the remaining legal requirements under the land laws.

12. Alice not only referred to herself as "The Pilgrim" but also used pseudonyms for her neighbors—"Ben Franklin" and "Isaac Newton," among the most obvious. The "Nash girls" were probably the Knox sisters, well-known residents and landholders in the Post area in the 1910s and 1920s. See Beverly A. Wolverton, *A Hundred and Sixty Acres in the Sage*. In Wolverton's anecdotal history of the Post area, many single women homesteaders are named, including several women who went on homesteading alone following the death of a husband. Casual references to women homesteaders are often abundant in local histories such as Wolverton's.

way, unhampered by what Mrs. So and So did or what Mrs. Somebody or other expected me to do."[13] Among them were many spinsters and widows looking for economic independence, either by farming on their own or by proving up on a claim, then selling out to someone for a grubstake to do something else.[14] Some were escaping from luckless marriages, either as divorcees or runaways. Many came West with other family members—sisters or parents, brothers or cousins—and filed claims in a block to gain family holdings as large as possible.[15] Some were hoping to earn a living outside the conventional women's realm, escaping work as schoolteacher, maid, or

---

13. A. May Holaday, "The Lure of the West for Women," *Sunset* 38 (March 1917), p.61.

14. In discussing the motivations of women homesteaders, I have largely followed Sheryll Patterson-Black, "Women Homesteaders on the Great Plains Frontier," and Sheryll and Gene Patterson-Black, "From Pack Trains to Publishing: Women's Work in the Frontier West," *Western Women in History and Literature* (Crawford, Nebraska: Cottonwood Press, 1978).

15. Alice's own family had broadened its holdings in Dakota when Grandfather Rand, at his son-in-law's urging, filed on 160 acres adjoining their homestead. Such homesteads were usually farmed cooperatively, with the individual family member meeting the residence requirement on his or her own. Richard Rand, for instance, lived in a little cabin the stipulated time to gain title to the land, though other requirements were apparently met by his daughter's family. Often, to ease the difficulty of separate residences, houses were built at or straddling the

factory worker.[16] At least a few women came West for reasons of health, either their own or members of their families', and saw in homesteading the only viable way to make the move. Some women had already tried to homestead at another location, or were second-generation homesteaders—Alice Pratt herself was spurred by a longing for the remembered "simple" life of her childhood in Mankato and Little Elk Canyon. And of course there were women who simply sought adventure—not a little of Alice's own motivation. "I had a haunting fear that it would be tame," she said (*Portfolio*, p.26).

---

common property line. In a telephone discussion, a man responding to my homesteading novel *The Jump-Off Creek* recounted the story of his mother and her three sisters who, he said, had filed on adjoining homesteads and built their houses all in a cluster at the intersection of the four corners of their individual claims.

16. Alice herself gave this as a reason for going West. "I have crossed the Rubicon," she wrote in *A Homesteader's Portfolio* (p.65). "On the thither side lie fifteen years of ardent schoolroom life, rows upon rows of little desks, the daily tension, the rigid schedule, principals amiable and crabbed, superintendents broadminded and arbitrary, school boards enlightened and ignorant, varying community requirements, social conservatisms, religious bigotries. For three years no binding contracts, no hours to keep, no patrons to please, no customs with which to conform, no conventionalities to respect, no standards to measure up to, no Mrs. Grundy to conciliate!"

It had been the Homestead Act of 1862 that had explicitly granted a woman, as well as a man, the right to file a claim for a homestead, provided she was single or head of a household, over 21 years of age, and a citizen or an immigrant who had filed papers to become a citizen. Over the next half century, the percentages of women among the claimants for homesteads increased steadily with the years, reaching their zenith in the 1910s when nearly one in five claims was filed by a woman—and the rate at which women gained title to their lands was apparently slightly better than men's.[17]

Yet homesteading women are substantially missing from the literature and histories of the West. American publishing, centered in the East, has presented Western women in popular literature in a sensationalized form—Calamity Jane, Belle Starr—or as "the long-suffering and essentially passive pioneer woman in sunbonnet who endured much but contributed little. . . ."[18] Sheryll Patterson-Black, in her study of women homesteaders on the Great Plains, points to the despondent and helpless wife, Beret Hansa, in O.E. Rolvaag's *Giants in the Earth*, as perhaps the

---

17. In the Patterson-Blacks' research of government land office records at Lamar, Colorado (for the representative years 1887 and 1907), and Douglas, Wyoming (1891, 1907, and 1908), 37 percent of men made final claim to the land, while 42.4 percent of the women succeeded.

18. Dorothy Gray, *Women of the West* (Millbrae, California: Les Femmes, 1976), p.3.

most common image of women on the American frontier, and interestingly notes that Rolvaag himself never homesteaded. Mari Sandoz and Willa Cather, by contrast—Sandoz born on a homestead, Cather a child of the Nebraska frontier—included among their fictional characters numerous independent and capable women, and several homesteader heroines. But the indelible image of Rolvaag's "reluctant pioneer" reverberates throughout Western fiction, eclipsing other images of women in the West, including the prairie fiction written by women such as Sandoz and Cather.

Historians seeking to widen this stereotypical view have recently begun turning to the writings of westering women themselves in order to discover who and what they were, but the scarcity of written accounts by homesteading women may be one reason for their continuing omission from histories of the period. The all-consuming effort of their work left most homesteading women without the time and energy for recording their experiences, their few published memoirs insufficient to offset the commonly held image of Western women as powerless and dependent helpmates.[19]

---

19. Many of the accounts that sound promising—such as Elinore Pruitt Stewart's well-known *Letters of a Woman Homesteader* were in fact written not by solitary women homesteaders but instead by women who homesteaded with their husbands, or by women recalling their childhood on a parental homestead. Of the few accounts by women who homesteaded alone—none providing as whole and representative a picture as Alice Pratt's—these are known to me:

Thus *A Homesteader's Portfolio* stands as an especially significant work, presenting not only a rare but an extraordinarily complete report of the life of a single-handed woman homesteader on a landscape fraught with peril and difficulty—a woman not the victim of her circumstances but taking her place as a part of history, and a maker of history.

*

In fact, Alice's eighteen year "experiment" in Oregon typifies homesteading experience—by both men and women—throughout the dry-land West. Her effort and failure epitomizes in particular the pattern of settlement on the Oregon high desert, where lay most of the lands opened to entry by the Enlarged Homestead Act of 1909.

Woman in Levis by Eulalia Bourne—a teacher who homesteaded in Arizona in the 1930s; *Shepherdess of Elk River* by Margaret Brown—a widow who continued homesteading after her husband's death in the 1910s; *No Life for a Lady* by Agnes Morley Cleveland—a childhood reminiscence, but the mother was a widow homesteading alone in New Mexico in the late nineteenth century; *Silence of the North* by Olive Frederick—a woman with three children, homesteading in British Columbia during the 1930s; *Land of the Burnt Thigh* by Edith Eudora Kohl—two sisters who homesteaded in South Dakota in the early 1900s; *Mountain Charley: The Adventures of a Woman Thirteen Years in Male Attire* by Charley O'Kieffe—not a homesteading account, but describes at some length her childhood experiences with a mother who homesteaded alone in Nebraska in the 1880s; *Bachelor Bess* by Elizabeth Corey—a collection of letters from a homesteader to

The early stream of settlers that flowed over the Oregon Trail beginning in the 1840s had passed straight across the Great Plains and the dry northeastern shoulder of Oregon without considering these lands fit for agriculture—they were intent on reaching the rich bottomlands of the Willamette river valley, the well-watered and wooded interior valleys of Western Oregon. But by the 1870s, as land-seekers found preferred areas already claimed, settlement began to rebound eastward across the Cascades.[20] The first Oregon-born generation, and latecomers from the East, began taking up tracts an earlier generation had turned their backs on. Stock raisers in particular moved onto watered lands wherever cattle and sheep could find adequate pasturage. But much of central Oregon, defined by high elevation and extremes of weather, as well as prevailing aridity, remained unsettled through the end of the nineteenth century. And when settlement finally came to this region after the turn of the century it was both swift and brief.

The "public domain"—land available for sale, entry and settlement under various provisions of United States homestead laws—was land once occupied by Native American peoples, and

---

her brother, over the years 1909-1919.

20. For three different views of the area's history, see Barbara Allen, *Homesteading the High Desert* (Salt Lake City: University of Utah Press, 1987); Raymond R. Hatton, *High Desert of Central Oregon* (Portland: Binford and Mort, 1977); and E.R. Jackman and R.A. Long, *The Oregon Desert* (Caldwell, Idaho: Caxton Printers, Ltd., 1964).

acquired by the federal government in cession from the original states, by "discovery," by treaty and purchase from foreign governments, and by treaty and usurpation from the tribes. Homestead laws varied over the years but generally allowed the head of a family to file a claim on a plot of land, usually 160 acres, and to gain ownership by paying a small filing fee and making certain "improvements"—clearing a portion of the land, erecting fence, building a home—and living on the land for a certain number of years. The Desert Land Act of 1891 had doubled the acreage that had been allowed under the provisions of the Homestead Act of 1862, but with the stipulation that the land be irrigated and producing a crop within three years. With the Enlarged Homestead Act of 1909, the onus of irrigation was removed, and in Oregon it was this change that opened a flood of settlement in the high desert east of the Cascades and south of the Blue Mountains.

The passage of the Enlarged Homestead Act came at a pivotal point.[21] Frederick Jackson Turner's declaration of the "closing of the frontier" had begun to sink into public consciousness by the turn of the century, and as the nation began an uneasy shift from a predominantly rural population to an urban one, two major pieces of conservation legislation set aside millions of acres

---

21. This discussion of the factors contributing to the surge of early twentieth-century homesteaders largely follows Barbara Allen, *Homesteading the High Desert.*

for national parks and forest reserves.[22] There was a widespread perception that the public domain would soon be gone, and the Back-to-the-Land movement, fervidly proclaiming the view that a life on the land was morally and physically more healthful than city life, was in part an emotional response to this perceived ending of a 300-year American "birthright." Within this general atmosphere of anxiety over the passing of the frontier and the dwindling supply of unreserved farmland, the prices for both land and agricultural products began to rise. At the same time, the introduction of mechanized equipment, chemical fertilizers, and "scientific" methods of cultivation—especially the advent of dry farming as a systematic set of farming practices—seemed to promise an extension of the limits of arable land. And in the wake of the panic of 1907, railroad promoters and Back-to-the-Land enthusiasts seeking to attract people to the arid lands of the West trumpeted their message to an audience of unemployed urban workers and recent foreign immigrants.

---

22. A provision in the Act to Repeal the Timber Culture Laws (March 3, 1891) authorized the President to withdraw public forest lands from entry, and to establish forest reserves by proclamation. It was an act without teeth until administration and protection of forest reserves were provided for by the Sundry Civil Appropriation Act (June 4, 1897). Between 1900 and 1910 more than 150 million acres were withdrawn from settlement. See E. Louise Peffer, *The Closing of the Public Domain: Disposal and Reservation Policies, 19009-1950* (Stanford: Stanford University Press, 1951).

In the midst of this flurry of change and anxiety, Americans answered the Enlarged Homestead Act as though it were a final summons. Nationally, more land was homesteaded in the twenty years after 1900 than in the forty years before. If the frontier were indeed passing from the American scene, here was one last chance to participate in it, and people who had never considered homesteading, along with those who had tried it more than once before, rushed to take up claims, even though lands opened to entry under the changed laws were at best the marginal remnants of the Western dream.

By her own report, Alice Day Pratt was spurred westward by a wish for an independent life, but undoubtedly there was an emotional component in her action as well. In *A Homesteader's Portfolio,* for instance, she imagines herself "afar on the prairies with the wind in my hair and the smell of new-plowed earth in every breath I drew. . . . Behind, what extremes of gayety [sic] and misery, what competition, what life at high pressure! Before, what calm, what freedom, what limitless spaces, what hope and opportunity!" (pp 2-3). In Alice's unpublished novel, *Sagebrush Fires,* as the heroine describes her father's vision of a home in central Oregon, Alice's own voice can perhaps be heard: "He dreamed of making an ideal home in the sagebrush country. He said civilization had gone very far wrong in many ways, getting farther and farther from Nature. He said that most of those that come into this life had been too hard pressed, have had no chance or opportunity to think about anything but making a living. . . . He wanted to help build up a community open-minded and truly progressive, founded on all the best that we know" (p.69).

For all their visionary hopes, even homesteaders with some experience of farming were daunted by the unfamiliar exigencies of the desert. "Locating" a suitable piece of land was a thriving business, and men as well as women seeking appropriate land for homesteading made use of their services. Representing themselves as knowledgeable about an area, locators advertised their expert advice for varying fees, hoping to attract the attention of landseekers like Alice Pratt who had come West without yet filing on a particular site.

The Crooked River valley, to which Alice's locator directed her, was one of several areas in central Oregon widely promoted for its potential as a future wheat-producing region. Newspapers throughout Crook and Lake counties frequently headlined plans for a railroad to connect Prineville to Redmond and Bend, and an extension of The Dalles-Bend route into California and across the desert to Lakeview and to Boise. Irrigation projects were expected to come to the region as a result of the U.S. Reclamation Act of 1902. Irrigation notwithstanding, rainfall on the central Oregon sagebrush lands was declared to be sufficient to grow wheat, with most promotional material and some U.S. Weather Bureau statistics putting the rainfall at ten to twenty inches yearly.[23] There was no reason for Alice to doubt that her

23. Allen, p.119.

locator had steered her toward one of the most promising areas of unreserved lands. And the base of Friar Butte, the particular site to which he brought her, must have recommended itself immediately: its "unfailing" spring assured necessary water in a region where water could never be taken for granted.

When she returned to the land office at Prineville to file her homestead entry, Alice claimed only 160 acres. Though most homesteaders were attracted to central Oregon by the publicity surrounding the Enlarged Homestead Act—and provisions of that act would have allowed entry to 320 acres—the residence requirement for a 160-acre claim under the original Homestead Act was three years rather than five, and a claim could be commuted, at $1.25 per acre, after residence of only fourteen months. Most entrymen filed, as Alice did, under the earlier provisions. Only after 1912, when the residence requirement under the Enlarged Homestead Act was relaxed from five years to three, did the number of enlarged homestead entries soar, and people like Alice who had already claimed 160 acres filed second claims, bringing their total holdings up to 320 acres.[24]

---

24. See Allen, pp.34-35, for a discussion of homesteaders' tendency to file under the older law. Alice mentions her second filing in *Portfolio*, p.116. Later, her growing herd of Jersey cows qualified her to double her allotment again—to 640 acres—under the provisions of the 1916 Stockraising Homestead Act, to which she makes a sidelong reference in *Portfolio*, p.180.

The law allowed a grace period of up to six months before a claimant had to take up residence on the claim. While some homesteaders used this time to build their houses before moving onto the homestead site, Alice was not uncommon in taking full advantage of the delay. After filing on the Broadview land, she finished out the school year teaching at Stanfield, and then entrained for Redmond.

Simply getting one's belongings to central Oregon was laboriously difficult. Then, as now, no railroads crossed the middle of the state. Alice, traveling from Pendleton, would have taken the Oregon-Washington Railroad and Navigation Company line, westbound as far as The Dalles, then south to Redmond; from Redmond, an auto stage crossed the twenty miles east to Prineville and brought her up the Crooked River valley another thirty miles to Post—a journey much the same as this one recounting a trip from Bend to Burns in 1913:

> *I thought I knew an automobile; but I found that I had never been on one of the Western desert breed. . . .The trail takes account of every possible bunch of sagebrush and greasewood to be met with on the way. It never goes over a bunch if it can go around a bunch; and as there is nothing but bunches all the way, the road is very devious. It turns, here and there, every four or five feet (perhaps the sagebrush clumps average five feet apart), and it has a habit, too, whenever it sees the homesteader's wire fences, of dashing for them, down one side of the*

claim, steering clear of all the clumps of sage, but ripping along horribly near to the sizzling barbs of the wire and the untrimmed stubs on the juniper posts; then darting into the brush, this way, that way, every way. . .[25]

When Alice and her belongings were finally deposited at the post office-store comprising the tiny community of Post, she was dependent on the generosity of neighbors, and her own "carrying power," for getting her goods across the last four miles to her homestead site at Friar Butte. It was weeks before all of her dunnage made its way across that last, formidable frontier.

Government publications and promotional literature candidly advised prospective homesteaders to bring enough capital with them for an initial outlay on stock, equipment, seeds, and building materials, and enough cash to cover living expenses until the first income-earning crop could be brought in. It was said that "any man with from 3,000 to 5,000 dollars capital who was not afraid of hardship and hard work could make the land support a family by the time the capital was expended."[26] But people with a substantial amount of capital could find more suitable land for purchase elsewhere—the irrigated Stanfield Project, for instance—and most arrived as Alice

25. Dallas Lore Sharp, *Where Rolls the Oregon* (Boston: Houghton Mifflin Co., 1914), pp.49-50.

26. Urling Coe, *Frontier Doctor* (New York: The Macmillan Co., 1939), p.227.

did, with little more than could be loaded on a wagon, or piled onto the auto stage.

Alice met her immediate need for shelter by pitching a tent—a conventional strategy for homesteaders. The task of building a home in the central Oregon desert was never easily accomplished—natural building materials were scarce, with juniper usually proving too small, too hard, and too crooked to be suitable for logs, and pine often protected in forest reserves or standing too far from desert building sites. Milled lumber was the most relied-upon material for houses and barns, but this often meant exorbitant shipping costs—lumber had to be brought by wagon over unimproved roads from mill sites sometimes days away. Alice Pratt was fortunate in the proximity of the pine-clad Maury Mountains, which enabled her to trade eggs for building materials at a sawmill only six miles from her building site. The house she eventually built with the paid help of her neighbors was typically small and simple, of box-frame construction, unpainted and sparsely furnished; its only unusual aspect may have been the attention she paid to the site—precisely locating her windows to take advantage of her favorite vista, the "ever changing hues" of the Blue Mountains to the East.[27]

Homestead law required that fencing be erected and crops sown, a development many stock ranchers who had settled in central Oregon

---

27. For an interesting description of the abandoned Broadview house some forty years later, see Clarine Silver, "The Old Maid of Friar Butte."

a generation earlier could only view with antipathy. Accustomed to grazing their cattle on the public domain, these "Old Oregonians," as Alice termed them, regarded the wave of twentieth-century homesteaders as an invasion. Alice's early naivete about ranchers' hostility to homesteaders is a wry subtext in *A Homesteader's Portfolio*. "It amuses me at this distance to picture what must have been the contrast between my unguarded and interrogative innocence and their shrewd reserve," Alice remarks from the "distance" of nearly ten years on the land (*Portfolio*, p.49). Many of her misfortunes, especially her chronic difficulties finding reliable farm help, were related to antagonism from ranchers. "The only way to deal with them homesteaders is to starve 'em out," remarks one of Alice's Old Oregonians. In writing for *The Atlantic Monthly* shortly after leaving Broadview in 1931—"seeking relief for the pain of my heart"—Alice could not quite conceal her bitterness.

> *The introduction of Jerseys into the heart of beef country was a presumptuous act and was, to some extent, treated accordingly. The fences of the region are not built to withstand the assault of a herd sire from either side. A strain of Jersey in a beef animal detracts from his weight and also renders him less able to withstand the rigors and hardships to which he is born. 'A bullet for the Jersey bull' might have been the slogan fifteen years ago. . . . The first calf that I destined for a herd sire was removed from the scene of action in his*

early infancy. Ann's Lad [a later bull] has bluffed it through, but carries at least one bullet and several scars as souvenirs of visits outside his proper range. On my side, I have become familiar with the aspect of every range bull in the vicinity. . . . One February evening, when snow lay deep, a huge Hereford, with horns like the traditional Texan, tore my barnyard gate to shreds, let seven horses in with him on to the last, small stack of hay that I was able to secure that year, tore several cows loose from their moorings in the shed, and occupied their quarters, in which I found him calmly reposing in the morning. What cattleman, if cases were reversed, would not have shot him where he lay? Yet intrusions upon the dairy herd receive little attention. . . . More than a score of whiteface calves have intruded themselves into my otherwise homogeneous herd, a better testimony than my complaints, to trespassing from without ("Jerseys," p.57).

For her friendships, Alice turned most often to other newly arrived homesteaders. Pie suppers, basket socials, holiday picnics and pageants, as well as impromptu outings, evenings of cards, singing, or dancing, were popular and frequent pastimes in homesteading communities throughout the West, and much in evidence in Alice's society of "hard-working bachelors." In a study of Fort Rock-Christmas Lake Valley homesteaders, Barbara Allen asserts that such "intense" socializing

> *afforded not only a welcome but a psychologically necessary diversion from the physical, emotional and economic hardships that desert life imposed on the homesteaders. Many had come from urban settings where amenities such as electric lights and indoor plumbing were taken for granted and had engaged in occupations far less physically demanding or economically precarious than farming. Even the people who had agricultural experience had to adapt themselves to the peculiar conditions of the high desert. Everyone had to cope with the extremes of heat and cold and inadequate protection from either, with cramped living quarters and a monotonous diet, with hard work and limited rewards for its accomplishment, with separation from former homes and friends and isolation from the world at large.*[28]

A Homesteader's Portfolio frequently suggests such needfulness—as when Alice describes a social event in the Basin as "one of those little dinners that are becoming quite the thing with a happy circle of us—friendly gatherings that make a strong appeal to the new and lonesome homesteader" (p.80).

At times she records plaintive journal entries of a more personal kind—her wistful desire to take in orphans, for instance, and her often conflicted views on love and marriage: "What sort of old maid am I anyway that I can't walk home in the moonlight with an attractive boy without tingling

28. Allen, pp.79-80.

from head to foot! Good reason why devoted hermits segregate themselves. In the peace of Broadview I haven't felt this way for lo these many moons" (*Portfolio*, p.92).

In fact, opportunities for marriage presented themselves—bachelors in the rural West viewed each succeeding school teacher as a possible wife—but she "fear[ed] the life-long bond." In writing years afterward of her winters at the Conant Basin school, Alice reported that "one handsome French man began at once in a business-like way, spending Sunday afternoons (such presious [sic] afternoons) with me. He brought, each time, a single vegetable as a present and as an example of his agriculture. He told me in a note that he 'had nottings' but that he would take good care of my 'stalk'. I switched my day of going to the valley [Broadview] from Saturday to Sunday. After he had called twice and found me absent, he took the hint" (*Trek*, Chapter 7, p. 11).[29] She was one of those, she said, "to whom the thought that spontaneity might become obligation is intolerable."

Homesteading was an arduous life for a single person, male or female. Once fenced, the

---

29. Barbara Allen reports an experience similar to Alice's, recorded in the diary of Anna Steinhoff, who homesteaded with her sister near Christmas Lake in 1910: "This afternoon one of the bachelor neighbors came. He brought me a rabbit and then told me of his hunt etc. We talked of very sensible subjects until dusk. Then his conversation drifted off on matrimony etc. I was honored with a proposal and he with a refusal before he left" (*Homesteading*, p.36).

land had to be cleared of sagebrush, and homestead law required that at least one-eighth of the acreage—five acres out of every forty—be under cultivation within three years. Turning sage and grasslands into productive farmland involved a good deal of back-breaking work, and most homesteaders undertook it within the context of a family, with success depending upon the physical labors of not only a husband and a wife—or brother and sister—but also children and other relatives, often parents, cousins, or in-laws.[30] Frequently, homesteaders traded work with their neighbors, helping one another to build a house or barn, to clear or fence a field, plow, or harvest a crop. Alice's solitariness may have been her most unusual condition. Being not only single but a woman, and utterly alone on her land, Alice was at a disadvantage in trying to reciprocate a neighbor's labor. With no "bank account" to draw on, she was often in straits when she needed a strong back to help with field work or building—a lament that rings throughout *A Homesteader's Portfolio.*

Even with the efforts of several family members, wresting a living from arid land was a difficult proposition at best, and nearly all those who took up homestead claims in the Oregon high desert had to look for a source of income other than the land itself. By the time a settler had

30. Sherry L. Smith, "Single Women Homesteaders: The Perplexing Case of Elinor Pruitt Stewart," *Western Historical Quarterly* (May 1991), XXII, 177-178. See also Allen , p.36, and Patterson-Black, p.26.

purchased lumber for a house, wire for fencing, supplies for the family, and seed for crops, little capital was left.[31] When their money gave out they found employment where they could, and this often meant spending at least a few months of each year at work away from their claims. While men were away working for wages, the women and children remained to plow, grub sagebrush, haul wood and water; adolescent children took work as hired girls or cowboys, seamstresses or carpenters, and contributed their wages to the family income.[32] The few single men and women like Alice, without other family members to help carry the load, were in an especially difficult situation. While her journal had joyously proclaimed a three-year freedom from "rows upon rows of little desks," Alice was quickly obliged to take a winter teaching position at the Post-Newsom school, and she spent the following winter at a Prineville school, living in a tent house at the edge of the town. When the third winter[33] came around and she realized that her still-

31. In fact, some families began to leave almost as soon as they had arrived. Barbara Allen was told of a settler who had left soon after building his house. "I had that much money and I spent it. And when I spent it there was nothing else to do." Allen's informant told her, "He couldn't live on nothing, so he left" (*Homesteading*, p.37).

32. For example, see Allen, pp.82-84, and Patterson-Black, p.26.

33. Alice referred to this as her "second winter," though it was in fact her third (*Portfolio*, p.120). She occasionally lapsed into such inaccuracies. In *Three*

unplanted wheat could be put to use supplying feed for the chickens, she "decided to stay by the place." Though she had hoped the gain from eggs would see her through, midwinter found her impoverished to the point of "lack[ing] two cents for postage." She turned to writing as a mean of supplementing her meager income: in the 1910s, two poems that would later appear in *A Homesteader's Portfolio* were sold to *Sunset*, and two articles made their appearance in *The Atlantic Monthly*. In 1922, The Macmillan Company brought out *A Homesteader's Portfolio*. At least one unpublished short story also dates from the 1920s. But throughout her eighteen years at Broadview, economic hardship continually drove her back to teaching, and she was often absent from the land in the winter months.[34] Her neighbors faced this situation as well, but Alice, as a bachelor without other family members on the land, had also the difficulty of seeing to the needs of her livestock, tending her fields and fences, and keeping up her buildings without a helping hand.

All across the arid West, homesteaders followed the methodology of dry farming: plowing

---

Frontiers she gave June 4 as the date of her arrival at Broadview, though in the earlier-written *A Homesteader's Portfolio* she had given June 30 as the date.

34. The homestead law made her seasonal absence allowable. In 1912, when the residence requirement for an enlarged homestead was relaxed from five years to three, a provision was added allowing a homesteader five months' absence from the claim each year.

deep, harrowing after each rain, increasing the organic matter in the soil, and fallowing half their fields in alternate years—procedures designed to trap moisture in the ground where it would be available for the growing plants. Dry farming had an ancient history, but its popularity in the United States in the first decades of this century grew from adaptations developed by H.W. Campbell around 1900, when he successfully introduced its use into Graham County in western Kansas, a region with fifteen-inch rainfall. One appeal of dry farming was its status as a scientific, up-to-date approach, and Alice reports "diligently studying" bulletins of state and county experiment stations for advice on dry farming techniques, and receiving both experimental seeds and advice from the "county agriculturist" —probably the U.S.D.A. County Agricultural Extension Agent, a program established in 1913. Though the U.S.D.A. in the 1910s was cautioning farmers against putting too much reliance on the "still experimental" dry farming techniques, the methods of dry farming were widely promulgated in several popular handbooks and in numerous articles that appeared in national and local newspapers. The Dry Farming Congress in particular —its membership made up of railroad executives, representatives of agricultural equipment manufacturers, and government and civic bureaucrats—was at work spreading rosy visions of what dry farming would accomplish in the arid regions. Seldom was much attention paid to actual tests and trials; dry farming promoters concentrated on promises of the future.[35]

---

35. Allen, pp.129-133.

While wheat was expected to be the primary cash crop among dry land farmers in central Oregon—and Alice also reports early efforts to grow field peas, Milo Maize, and alfalfa—her first plowed ground was given over to a vegetable garden. Virtually all homesteaders, cash-poor and facing high prices for scarce goods at desert stores, cleared just enough land in the first year to grow foodstuffs for their own families. In addition, nearly everyone kept chickens as food for the table. Where there were local markets for egg sales, chickens could also be a supplement to income, and Alice's full-fledged chicken operation, utilizing the most modern methods of incubation and enjoying a home market just six miles away among the "good sized force" at the sawmill, was "the one materialized hope of my adventure." The milk, cream, and butter from dairy cattle were another common source of both food and cash, though Alice declared her own dairy herd "has not been commercially successful."

> *In the spring and early summer these slopes are ideal as Jersey pasture. Probably no succulent feed surpasses young bunch grass in milk production. When the inevitable drought comes on, early or late, milk begins to fail, and I must look for watered fields, and haystacks that are the product of irrigated lands. . . . To keep my Jerseys, I have taught during parts of most years, earning the disrespect of my business-minded friends, the disgust of banks and loan companies that have, from time to time, seen me through the dubious*

experiment, and for myself, gray hairs, calloused hands—and some intangibles ("Jerseys," p.52).

She counted among those intangibles the "gentle response of these calm and friendly creatures that soothes the spirit and leaves the mind free for its own excursions. Not so with the harassing companionship of non-understanding humans" (*Portfolio,* p. 138). Alice's written work very often reflects this fond attachment to "the lower orders": all five of Pratt's *Atlantic Monthly* essays, both of her books written for children, and long portions of her two published books of memoirs concern themselves with animals, and reveal an emotional sensibility that may have derived from her mother, who she said "entered into the experiences of our wild neighbors and pitied them in their vicissitudes" (*Frontiers,* p.4). In this, as in her single-handedness, Alice seems to stand apart from other homesteaders. Though her idealism led her to hope that a "developing sensibility . . . will deliver us from the stockyards and the habit of feeding upon our fellow creatures" ("Jerseys," p.53), she was grimly aware of the homesteaders' and stockmen's common treatment of animals. "Toward other species than the human, principle and practice were hard and rigorous. Exploitation for human profit was the only recognized use of 'the beasts that perish' and a naive astonishment greeted any other viewpoint. Hunting and trapping were the pastimes of the winter season, and killing was the appropriate human reaction to the phenomena of animate existence" (*Portfolio,* p. 45).

For herself—even in her relations with destructive plagues of jackrabbits, and chicken-eating hawks—Alice practiced a compassionate conservation ethic, undertaking to protect her animals and fields by the most minimal, least torturous methods, and taking thoughtful stock of her own ecological impact on the desert: "For a thousand years, presumably, this vast plateau which is now my home has been covered with sage-brush and bunch grass and sprinkled with juniper trees, and has supported a normal population of jack rabbits and sage rats. Then suddenly comes man with his alien stock, his dogs and his cats, his new and succulent crops, with their admixture of weed seeds and germs of insect life. And lo, this quiet and harmonious state of nature is all in turmoil" (*Portfolio*, p. 144).[36]

Her inclination toward the perspective of animals seemingly gave her a clear-eyed view of the human place in natural history. "How Nature should smile over our little arrogancies and proprietorships! Even the dinosaurs dominated the earth for only a hundred million years or so! And only a bone here and there records their enormous size and strength" (*Frontiers*, p.53). This wry observation takes on a particular poignancy in light of Alice's own experience homesteading in

36. Alice made a similar remark about Little Elk Canyon: "We as a family were never ruthless toward the earlier inhabitants of the canyon. In fact, we protected and improved the fortunes of many of them. Yet our coming made it certain that ultimately these murmuring woods would yield to the uses of man" (*Frontiers*, p.41).

the arid West, for the buoyant optimism and energetic growth in central Oregon in the early years of the twentieth century gave way quickly to poverty, defeat, and flight. By 1916—only six years after the peak of homestead entries in the West—the homesteading boom was already over, and by 1920 a wholesale exodus had cut the desert population by more than half. Abandoned homesteaders' houses ghosted the central Oregon landscape. Only one of every five and a half entries went to final proof,[37] and by 1940, 65 percent of the land claimed under the Enlarged Homestead Act had reverted to the federal government.[38]

A string of factors contributed to this swift reversal, but most notable among them was the weather.[39] Throughout much of the West, several relatively wet and mild years coincided with the rush of homesteaders. Weather records were not kept before the arrival of the homesteaders in the 1900s, but average rainfall around Bend in the years 1902-1912 was nearly three inches above

---

37. Peffer, p.144.

38. Allen, citing James Slama Buckles, "The Historical Geography of the Fort Rock Valley, 1900-1941" (M.A. thesis, University of Oregon, 1959), p.108.

39. This discussion of the factors leading to the demise of homesteading in central Oregon derives from Barbara Allen, *Homesteading the High Desert*; Raymond Hatton, *High Desert of Central Oregon* (Portland: Binford and Mort, 1977); and E.R. Jackman and R.A. Long, *The Oregon Desert* (Caldwell, Idaho: Caxton Printers, 1964).

what would later prove to be the long-term average, and only two years of the next six were below the norm.[40] The average number of frost-free days was also generally favorable during the first few years after the passage of the Enlarged Homestead Act. These salutary conditions, combined with the deceptive productivity of the virgin soil, temporarily nourished the hopes and expectations of homesteaders all across the West.[41] For a time, nearly every 320-acre parcel from Bend to Burns and from Prineville to Lakeview was occupied and individually farmed. Under the impetus of the "new" system of dry farming, thousands of acres of land that had been exclusively range country were entered and put to the plow—and only then did the limitations of dry farming reveal themselves, with crop yield even during this favorable weather period falling below the level necessary to successfully support a family. When the weather after 1916 began to return to its drier and colder standard, homesteaders with little or

---

40. Hatton, *Desert*, pp.31-32.

41. Alice, in writing of her childhood in Little Elk Canyon, declared, "Every pioneer farmer proves the superiority of new soil, especially for root crops. . . . As one example out of many, I might cite an historic potato: one day we boiled and mashed a potato from a neighbor's garden for our family dinner—the family at that time numbering five. What was left of that potato was fried for breakfast the next morning. What was left over from breakfast was consigned to the retainers of other species. And this potato was not particularly outstanding among the first root vegetables of the new soil!" (*Frontiers*, p.34).

no reserves to sustain them began to give up their farms.[42] R. A. Long and E. R. Jackman—"Old Oregonians" with long-time roots in the area—wrote that "It usually took five years for a man to arrive, build a house, fence some land, break it, put in a crop, wait in vain to harvest it, lose his money, get tired of jack rabbit stew, and leave."[43]

Those who stayed, including Alice Pratt, faced a succession of worsening blows. Irrigation and cultivation, by drawing salts to the surface, aggravated the natural alkalinity of the desert soils, and the fine dry topsoil in fallow fields blew away on the wind, sometimes to a depth of two or three feet.[44] Diminishing precipitation was quickly reflected in the lowering levels of wells, while the clearing of willows and sage from nearby slopes caused springs to begin to silt. Jack rabbits, which had troubled the homesteaders in their fields and gardens from the beginning, became an intolerable plague. They swarmed over the fields by the thousands and stripped the tender new shoots of wheat, lettuce, and peas as fast as the growth appeared. Wheat that survived the ravages of

---

42. "Good years aren't expected here," wrote R.A. Long, whose family had been among the first to range cattle in the high desert. "Normally we don't count crops by tons, feet in height, or bushels to the acre—if they are alive, they are a success. . . . A homestead is supposed to be farmland—but the desert isn't farmland. Rainfall can drop to as low as five inches in a year, which won't raise any known crop" (*Oregon*, pp.44 and 46).

43. Jackman and Long, p.319.

44. Allen, p.109.

rabbits turned yellow with the onset of hot, dry weather and withered before it could head out. Though the rail line connecting Prineville with Redmond was finally put through in 1918, lines that had been expected to connect them to markets in California and Boise failed to materialize, as did promised irrigation projects. Expensive "heavy teaming" continued to be necessary to get supplies into the country and the grain crops back to the railway. By the time the bottom fell out of the wheat market in the agricultural depression of the early 1920s, half the homesteaders were already gone and the communities that had grown up around them were already disappearing.

Still, Alice Pratt hung on. The string of dry years continued unabated into 1925, and the winter of 1924-25 was a particularly hard one. In her unpublished manuscript, *Teacher's Trek*, Alice, who was then living and teaching at Maury school, twenty miles east of Post on the Crooked River, reported a memorable storm.

> *"The next morning we came together in a blinding snowstorm. It was not very cold, but the storm was difficult to breast. All day it drove and whistled against the south wall of the school house. Snow piled up on that side to the upper sashes of the windows. We worked in a soft twilight. It lay across the road in huge, packed drifts. We were warm and cosey [sic] in our well-built school house, with plenty of piney wood. We prosecuted our regular tasks and practiced the Christmas program diligently, but we*

were rather sober. All of the business interests of my pupils' families were 'live' interests and—sad to say—unsheltered."

That night, calves who had sought protection in the bare willow thickets along the river were crying in the night. The next day was the coldest of her life, thirty-three degrees below zero at mid-morning. Alice trudged out to see her young roosters. In a passage that seems to echo that childhood story of her frost-bitten ears, she wrote,

> *"The twenty young cocks, as white as the snow drifts, sat starkly upon their perches as if enchanted. There was a statuesqueness about them that sent a chill over me, cold as I was. No, they were not dead, but thos [sic] wattles that characterize their breed were as hard and stiff as plaster. Their feet were not frozen. It was the evening dip in the water dish that had done the mischief. Dabbling in the water had started the freezing before the night's cold had found them. Full-feeding was all that had saved the flock from death."*

Tramping back through the drifts, she was struck by

> *"The appearance of the little house, lost in the wilderness of snow, and fringed with icicles almost to the ground. . . . Sometimes, in the doubly walled shelter of a steam-heated apartment building I wake on a midwinter night and wonder whether the little house still stands in a wilderness of*

snow, and whether little calves are crying in the willows" (Trek, Chapter 8, pp. 3-9).

The following spring was early and wet, but when another dry cycle began in 1928 and persisted into the 1930s, overlapping the widening economic depression of that decade, the death knell was sounded for Alice Pratt's adventure at Broadview. In the spring of 1930 the loan company took possession of her Jerseys, and finally the herd was sold for exactly the amount of the loan.[45] Alice gave away her chickens to the old friends whose ranch adjoined hers, asking them to tend her land and care for her ponies "as long as they lived."[46] And at the close of 1930 she left the Broadview house for the last time.

---

45. Brooks Ragen cites letters from Alice to her mother, March 30, 1930, and June 15, 1930, telling of an unauthorized sale made by the third party pasturing the cows: "Laddie [Ann's Lad, her longtime herd sire] and the heifers went for beef, which is not so bad from a business standpoint as it might seem, since a great deal of good dairy stock is going that way. [But] It's all cruel and horrible to me at the best. I simply have to take it as one of the horrors of the world 'the way it is'." Ragen also cites an unpublished short story, "Depression on the Rimrock," in which Alice wrote feelingly of a rancher watching his cows loaded on trucks bound for the slaughterhouse in Portland: "Every creature on the place had been a friend of the family. Death, when it must come, had been a terrible necessity. . . . When their rich usefulness was past, they should be killed expertly right here on the place, with no experience of apprehension or unkind handling."

46. Writing shortly after she had left Broadview, Alice

*

"The homesteading era was pathetic, I suppose," wrote E.R. Jackman. "Eastern schoolteachers were the most notable group. They came with a dreamy, mystical approach, hopelessly impractical."[47] He put forward Alice Day Pratt—"an old maid schoolteacher from New York"—as a kind of proof, by citing without comment a particularly flowery passage from *A Homesteader's Portfolio.*[48] But in fact, Alice had managed to hang on to her "homesteading dream" more than a decade after most other homesteaders had packed their belongings and left the desert—this despite her solitariness and meager resources. She had tramped afoot as much as six miles daily to her school post in every kind of weather; had ridden

---

expressed the hope that her remaining horses and ponies "may live out their lives upon this solitary butte, haunting the south side in the winter season and the north side in summer, tasting the wine of spring in the ripened seed, hiding beneath juniper canopies from the driving storms, and seeking the first rays of morning on the pinnacle of the hill . . ." ("Hippos," p.743).

47. Jackman and Long, p.52.

48. Jackman selected: "The possession of ancestral acres is bound up with sentiment, yet—virgin soil bestows an inspiration of its own. How the centuries have toiled through fire and frost and wind and wave and springing life and long decay to lay their fields so wide and deep. They alone among the fields of earth have suffered neither neglect nor ignorance nor folly. Reverent as Adam we should come to them" (*Portfolio*, p.114-115).

weekly as much as sixty miles roundtrip to Broadview in order to meet the residence requirement on her property; had single-handedly tossed and stacked 100,000 pounds of hay—"twenty five tons lifted twice"—even as her friends on nearby homesteads were giving up and going off to other endeavors. She had withstood repeated crop failures, depredations of range cattle and jack rabbits, the hostility and larceny of her ranching neighbors—and perhaps would have been wryly amused to hear Jackman's characterization of her as dreamy. She had herself once criticized Hamlin Garland as a man who "was no born farmer. He lacked the tastes and appreciation that are the alleviations of the hardships of farming" ("Jerseys" p.55).[49] In her view, it was the capacity to dream—to "be a child again—a child of the desert"—that made sense of the harsh realities of the homesteading experience. Her feeling for both the landscape and the life of the farm sprang not from dreamy mysticism but from long, practical experience, lived close upon the land.

The last third of *Three Frontiers* was virtually a reissue of *A Homesteader's Portfolio*, with lengthy portions taken verbatim from the earlier work. But Alice Pratt's closing comment in *Three Frontiers* was written from more than twenty years

---

49. Interestingly, Garland was among the Western Writers discussed by Sheryll Patterson-Black in her essay "Women Homesteaders on the Great Plains Frontier." She pointed out his espousal of women's causes, and contrasted it with his use of the "reluctant pioneer" imagery in *Son of the Middle Border*.

remove. "Now, in 1953, I would add this word that experience has made clear to me: Success may be the smallest and least important of the fruits of endeavor; it is the endeavor itself, the opportunity to use one's whole self completely—initiative, creativity, and physical strength—that is its own reward: and it may well be that one looks back upon the times of greatest strain and anxiety as the high points in [one's] pilgrimage" (p. 132).

Barbara Allen, remarking on the widespread inclination among historians and other writers to dismiss the twentieth-century homesteaders as "at best shortsighted and at worst benighted fools," wrote that "Either judgement is, of course, grossly unfair to what the homesteaders did, why they did it, and what their acts ultimately meant."[50]

Alice Day Pratt in *A Homesteader's Portfolio*—exploring what she did and why she did it—shines a rare light on a signal event in the history of the American West. Her life at Broadview illuminates not only the powerfully defining American dream of land ownership, but women's stake in that dream. And for the meaning in Alice Pratt's life, we may do well to look at the landscape of her own frontier myth—at the intersection where her independent spirit and tacit feminism converge with the ideals of the Back-to-the-Land movement and a conservationist ethos. "I have been cold and hungry and ragged and penniless," she said. "I have been free and strong and buoyant and glad."

---

50. Allen, p.140.

An Alice Day Pratt Bibliography

"Song of the Homesteaders" (poem). *Sunset* 31 (August 1913).

"Heritage" (poem). *Sunset* 34 (March 1915).

"Feathered Affection" (in admiration of barnyard fowl and birds in general). *The Atlantic Monthly* (April 1915).

"White Leghorns" (description of her chicken venture at Broadview). *The Atlantic Monthly* (July 1916).

A Homesteader's Portfolio (memoir). New York: The Macmillan Company, 1922.

"Jerseys" (thoughtful commentary on her Broadview cows and dairy animals in general). *The Atlantic Monthly* 147 (January 1931).

"Hippos" (thoughtful commentary on her Broadview ponies and horses in general). *The Atlantic Monthly* 147 (June 1931).

Animals of a Sagebrush Ranch (juvenile). New York: Rand McNally, 1931.

"I Take to the Woods" (rhapsodic description of three woodland experiences including one on the Oregon coast). *The Atlantic Monthly* 150 (September 1932).

Animal Babies (juvenile). Beacon Press, 1941.

Three Frontiers (memoir). New York: Vantage Press, 1955.

Several unpublished manuscripts are in the keeping of Walden Penfield Pratt, Arvada, Colorado.

Bibliography

Allen, Barbara. *Homesteading the High Desert.* Salt Lake City: University of Utah Press, 1987.

Coe, Urling C. *Frontier Doctor.* New York: The Macmillan Co., 1939.

Gray, Dorothy. *Women of the West.* Millbrae, Calif.: Les Femmes, 1976.

Hatton, Raymond R. *High Desert of Central Oregon.* Portland: Binford and Mort, 1977.

Holaday, A. May. "The Lure of the West for Women" *Sunset* 38 (March 1917).

Jackman, E.R. and R.A. Long. *The Oregon Desert.* Caldwell, Idaho: Caxton Printers, Ltd., 1964.

Jensen, Joan M. *With These Hands: Women Working the Land.* New York: The Feminist Press, 1981.

Patterson-Black, Sheryll and Gene. *Western Women In History and Literature.* Crawford, Nebraska: Cottonwood Press, 1978.

Peffer, E. Louise. *The Closing of the Public Domain: Disposal and Reservation Policies 1900-1950.* Stanford: Stanford University Press, 1951.

Ragen, Brooks. "Alice Day Pratt in Oregon." Unpublished manuscript. 37 pp. Seattle, 1976.

Sharp, Dallas Lore. *Where Rolls the Oregon.* Boston: Houghton Mifflin Co., 1914.

Silver, Clarine. "The Old Maid of Friar Butte." *Eugene Register-Guard* (April 23, 1972).

Smith, Sherry L. "Single Women Homesteaders: The Perplexing Case of Elinore Pruitt Stewart." *Western Historical Quarterly* XXII (May 1991).

Wolverton, Beverly A. *A Hundred and Sixty Acres in the Sage: Homestead History of the Immediate Post Area.* Post, Oregon: Beverly Wolverton, 1984.

A HOMESTEADER'S PORTFOLIO

THE MACMILLAN COMPANY
NEW YORK · BOSTON · CHICAGO · DALLAS
ATLANTA · SAN FRANCISCO

MACMILLAN & CO., LIMITED
LONDON · BOMBAY · CALCUTTA
MELBOURNE

THE MACMILLAN CO. OF CANADA, LTD.
TORONTO

A HOMESTEADER'S PORTFOLIO

BY

ALICE DAY PRATT

New York
THE MACMILLAN COMPANY
1922

All rights reserved

PRINTED IN THE UNITED STATES OF AMERICA

COPYRIGHT, 1922,
BY THE MACMILLAN COMPANY.

Set up and printed. Published October, 1922.

Press of
J. J. Little & Ives Company
New York, U. S. A.

CONTENTS

SONG OF THE HOMESTEADERS

Serried and sharp is the region's rim
Like lunar cliffs clear-cut and bold,
Plains under quivering waves of heat,
Plains under fierce, untempered cold.
Dreary the landscape, lichen-gray,
Sage brush and juniper miles on miles.
Never a wood bird whistles gay,
Never a violet peeps and smiles.
Coyote and jack rabbit, wolf and owl,
Prairie dog, eagle, and rattlesnake.
Bones of the bison and starveling steer
Season on season bleach and bake.

Whirling dust storm and shifting sand—
This, oh this, is the Promised Land!

Silvery, sinuous, ditch and flume
Leading down, from the arid steep,
Water of life to the land below—
Virginal valleys rich and deep.
Limitless orchards of peach and plum
Checking the landscape east and west,
Garden and vineyard and soft-eyed herds,
And woolly flocks with abundance blessed.
Barn and haystack and bungalow
And blaze of flowers for the passerby,
And soldierly ranking of poplar spires
Silhouette on the sunset sky,

And sweet-breathed meadows a billowy sea—
This is the Country-That-Is-To-Be!

A HOMESTEADER'S PORTFOLIO

I

THE ADVENTURE

ABOUT the year nineteen-ten came to me—teacher and spinster—the conviction that Fate had paid me the compliment of handing over the reins. She had failed to provide for me that ideal relationship which alone is the basis of the true home, and I was by nature obdurate toward accepting anything less at her hands. When a youthful friend was surreptitiously chidden for using the term "old maid" in my presence, the incident gave rise to thought. What now? I asked myself. *Quo vadis,* old maid? What will you do with life? Perhaps you have known the glory and the dream. Will you subsist henceforth upon the memory thereof or shall life continue to be for you that "ecstasy" "nothing less than which is worthy of the name"?

But by what route, if any, was that ecstasy to be attained? Not in the character of an "unplucked rose on the ancestral tree"—an illustration of the immemorial dependence and subjection of the feminine. Not through that occasional achievement—"fifty years a teacher." The road that led that way was far too closely hedged about by organization, boards, principals, superintendents, wise and otherwise parental interference, for any satisfying and permanent results. Not through social service as I knew it in the great city. The slum missionary with a country heart is far more truly a subject for charity than little Paolo and Francesca in the tenement of a thousand souls. One's course, to be most effective, must be in line with one's spontaneous loves and interests.

For some months, while work went on as usual, I reflected deeply, and gradually evolved the determination to be a creative farmer. There recurred to me the longing and ambition—innate but hitherto suppressed—to own a portion of the earth's crust in my own right and to tamper with it unrestrained. I would build a farm, whereon I could exercise my delight in all forms of nature life and to which in time I might bring some little unparented children, on whom to wreak my educational convictions and whom I might hope some day to turn over—a little bunch of good citizens—to my native land.

My fellow teachers wondered somewhat that winter at my unaffected cheerfulness under certain afflictions that visited themselves upon us. They never dreamed that I was all the time afar on the prairies with the wind in my hair and the smell of new-plowed earth in every breath I drew.

From the Department of the Interior I obtained facts as to public lands—for I had no treasure laid up wherewith to buy. Anyway, the virgin soil suited my plan. My farm was to be a true creation.

Gradually the prospective field narrowed itself until I had decided upon Oregon. Then, that I might not be a pauper immigrant, I decided to procure a school in the state and take what time might be required for finding my waiting acres. Through the State Superintendent, rather late, I obtained a position as primary teacher in the little town of Athena, eastern Oregon, and, on one memorable September day, companioned by an inseparable brown dog, I found myself about to embark upon the great adventure.

"Portland, Oregon? To your left. Leaves in twenty seconds." The forbidding gate clanged to behind me and I sped down the track.

"Portland, Oregon? Right here. Mind the step, Madam. All aboard!" The conductor and his little stool swung themselves up behind me and the fast train for the Pacific coast moved noiselessly out of our great metropolis. Behind, what extremes of gayety and misery, what competition, what life at high pressure! Before, what calm, what freedom, what limitless spaces, what hope and opportunity! I had become a homesteader!

Out of Manhattan, out through garden-like suburbs bright with velvet lawns and asters and scarlet sage, through golf links and country clubs, slowly climbing into high and woodsy places where belated summer people thronged the platforms and plodded along the dusty roads. Over the mountains and down again through mining camps and iron towns blazing their flashlights to the sky. Out into lovely old farm lands whose fields and vineyards creep to within a stone's throw of a white-capped inland sea—and the farm-house windows look on both. Out into the dear, familiar Middle West, with its boundless undulating tide of crops and crops and crops, its Lombardies and its windmills, its roomy, hospitable homes and spacious barns—homes sheltering the bent and withered parents of college-bred sons and daughters.

In and out of the smoky shroud of a great city; over the river and into the corn lands—corn and corn and corn, a day of corn! Corn on the stalks for miles and miles, corn in huge, golden pyramids upon the ground, corn in wagons, corn in cars, corn in towering warehouses. Once, in a prairie of corn, the train came to a sudden halt and there was an altercation vigorous but brief. A fellow traveler, who had stolen out to investigate, came back laughing and explained that it was "bums." "Bums on top, underneath, and all over us," he testified. "The conductor's shaking them here where they can get a job if they want it. Don't seem to take to the idea much." He had brought back with him two or three sample ears of corn which he measured upon his arm —the full length of the lower arm from elbow to finger tips—"American gold," he commented, stroking the polished ranks of seed.

Somewhere in this borderland also we were flagged at a crossroads where was a sign bearing the legend "Rawhide." "Yes, bragged that he'd kill the first chief he met," related a neighbor, "down-East boy, just a youngster, he was. That's where he met his man. The tribe stayed their march just long enough to tack up his skin on a tree that grew where that sign stands."

And, suddenly, with daylight of the third morning, there is a change. We have slept in the old land and waked in the new. The sun comes up in red-gold majesty above a lofty, untamed, illimitable land that sweeps ever upward in bold, bare reaches to its crown of bold, bare mountain summits, unsoftened by foliage, undimmed by distance—clear-cut as the mountains of the moon. The Northwest —the great plains, the land of wild-west romance and cowboy domination! Early in the gray dawn of this morning I hear across the aisle in eager girl tones, "Mother, Mother, guess what place this is! Medicine Bow! and there is a hotel over there called 'The Virginia.' Oh, my!"

Up on the highest point of the railroad, eight

thousand feet above sea level, where many miles of gigantic snowsheds tell of abomination of desolation in the winter season, something caused a few moments' halt and the passengers got out and walked beside the train. In sparkling draughts from the direction of the dawn, came that atmosphere that brings life to the lifeless—champagne-like, intoxicating! Eastward to the golden morning, westward to the soft-toned horizon, northward and southward the view was limited but by the eye's own mechanism. In every direction one might ride for days without guide and without trail. Standing bareheaded on the heights, filled with new plans and with new hopes, one pilgrim surrendered herself to the spirit of the West!

At noon of the fourth day out, the conductor walked the train with jovial apology, announcing a holiday for the purpose of attending the circus. In fact the train would be held up for five hours at Pendleton and every one could go to the "Roundup." What was the Roundup? Why, an annual wild-west show characteristic of the country. No one, having seen it, would regret the delay. There was many-hued disappointment among the passengers, but, on the whole, amused and curious acceptance of the circus idea, and all turned out into the bustling, dingy streets of Pendleton.

II

THE ROUNDUP

THE dingy streets of Pendleton, on this final and great day of the show, were filled with a seething and motley multitude. There had been a street parade and its elements passed hither and yon on various errands, mingling with guests from a dozen states who had honored the event with their presence. Dashing western gentlemen—officers of the day—sheriffs and mayors and private citizens, galloped this way and that, making arrangements for the afternoon. Young buckaroos in outlandish chaps—black and white, crimson, mustard-colored and green—paraded with due importance, three or four abreast. Here and there a group elicited loud applause from the bystanders. Women of all grades, from pretty ladies in handsome riding costume to savage-looking squaws bare-headed and blanketed, made common holiday. Scores of spectators crowded about a harness-maker's window in which were displayed the gold-and-silver-inlaid saddle and the jeweled bridle—prizes to be awarded the champion of the buckaroos and of the equestriennes. Evidently there was no nooning on this festive day. Lunches were hastily snatched from booths on the street, and the crowd melted from the thoroughfare to reappear in the great outdoor amphitheater, which, by one o'clock, was packed to the last seat on the bleachers.

Five hundred horses chafed at the gates; one hundred wild-eyed young steers tossed their horns in the enclosures; the band played intermittently and the feet of the expectant crowd beat time upon the benches. In the arena, the water wagons prepared the ground, and that ubiquitous black-eyed horseman of the official decoration—the goal of numberless feminine eyes—the marshal of the Roundup—sped his deputies hither and yon. Above all hung that indescribable, diamond-dust western sky, swept by fleeces of cloud soft as the down on the breast of a swan. Near at hand, low, rock-rimmed hills enclosed this new-world drama from all the world without.

The trumpet blast, the instant parting of the great gates, the forward leap of the leaders of the grand parade, and in they come—gallant gentlemen and dainty misses of the western metropolis, browned ranch maids and buckaroos, male and female champions of the ranges, sullen squaws in rainbow garb and resplendent savages in paint and feathers. Varied as the hues of their habiliments are the riders, yet exhibiting without exception that one gift in common—the careless command of the horse and saddle. While the audience roars itself hoarse for its favorites, they ride below in proud and smiling nonchalance. The broad felt hat is raised to this hail and to that. The gauntleted hand flies up in joyous salute to neighbors and home folks on the benches. One guesses how many days of ranch-house drudgery have been lightened for that smiling maiden by the thought of this day when, with new riding suit and saddle, she will ride with the youth of her choice in the Roundup at Pendleton, or, during how many solitary nights on the plains that champion has pictured the face that shall witness his triumph in the Pendleton arena.

On the benches, alert and keen-eyed western citizens, professional men late from eastern universities, grizzled ranchers and homesteaders, and many a king of wheat and of cattle claim their share in the grace and new-world chivalry, the dauntless courage and conquest of Nature represented there below. Little wrinkled grandmothers scramble to their feet and cackle congratulations to Buddy or Sissy for whom they once played cock horse back there in the old ranch kitchen. Sunburned ranch mothers claim proprietary interest in "Buck" and "Hank," who have herded their husbands' steers. A continuous round of applause accompanies each of half a dozen champions as he makes the circuit. Hat in hand and smiling, rides Buffalo Vernon, king of the rangers, indomitable tamer of the cayuse and the steer. A slender woman—Mrs. Dell Blanchett —spares one hand from the management of her careering horse to answer a thousand plaudits. The Indians, proud and stoical, greet the uproar of the spectators with hideously striped and stony visages.

The parade disposed of, the program leads up gently from less violent feats of horsemanship to the grand climax—the bucking scene. The slender son of a ranger has trained three little grays to act in response to his touch and voice with the precision of a mechanical toy. Neck to neck, with even, unbroken gait, they trot, gallop, and leap the hurdle, while the young master stands lightly with a moccasined foot on either outside horse, the third running beneath the arch of his limbs. There is a cowboy race abounding in right-about turns and breakneck maneuvers, that call for the sure-footedness of a cat and the agility of an ape. There is a girls' relay race—three times round, change horses each time and saddle your own—in which an agile slip of a girl, with a bunch of curls tied in her neck, is about to win in the final round. Suddenly her horse bolts, crashes into the fence, falls and flings his rider headlong into the pen of steers. The hush of horror is broken only by a deafening strain of applause, when, up, mounted, and passing her mates with a backward smile, she reaches the goal an easy length ahead. Next, he who can run down his steer, rope, throw, and hog-tie him in the minimum number of seconds, comes in for his reward. Buffalo Vernon must show how, unaided save by his own native strength, he can fling himself from his horse upon the neck of a racing steer, conquer, bring him to earth, and hold him there with his teeth, raising both hands to the crowd above the prostrate captive.

The broncho-busters' contest to-day is the grand climax not only of the day's program but of the three days' show, the most desperate horses having been reserved, and the successful contestants of the preceding days being elected to ride them. Each candidate is provided with an untried horse, and both brute and human, as if conscious of their responsibility to the expectant throng, rise magnificently to the occasion. There is one new and final feature. There remains an unconquered broncho—a horse unsuccessfully attempted on the two preceding days. It happens that Joe Raley alone among the contesting buckaroos has not yet essayed to ride him, and now there are cries from the spectators of "Raley! Raley! Let the youngster try him. Let Raley ride him." Raley comes forward from the group of contestants and removes his hat, bowing to the crowd.

And now at length *he* stands—the observed of all observers—in the center of the arena—the Outlaw, the rebel, the man-hating, untamable cayuse! He is held at halter's length by a man on horseback.

He stands stiffened, braced, with all four feet apart, his head drawn back. He is approached only on horseback. Two horsemen ride up quietly one on either side. Gently and with infinite deliberation they draw the blind over his eyes. From now on he is motionless, save for a trembling that possesses him wholly—a seemingly cold, stark terror of man and his ways. A man on the ground passes the saddle—high-backed, two-cinched, equipped with bucking rolls—to the horseman on the left. The horseman transfers it by imperceptible degrees to the back of the Outlaw. The man on the ground, reaching beneath the ridden horse, places the straps in the cinch rings and passes them to the horseman, who draws them up, inch by inch, inch by inch, to a vise-like tightness. He then gives the signal to the waiting buckaroo. Now Joe Raley steps forward between the Outlaw and the ridden horse on the left. With a quick movement he places his foot in the stirrup and swings himself to the saddle, his right foot dropping as if by instinct into its place. The horsemen on either side, having removed the halter, back quickly away, drawing off the blind. The Outlaw is left without bridle or halter. The rider raises both hands to the benches in token of good faith. He must not "touch leather" during the trial. He pulls off his hat and strikes the horse upon the shoulder.

The Outlaw, the vision of the vast human herd

being suddenly laid bare before him, sits back upon his haunches as if confronting a specter. Then he rises slowly upon all fours and then on two feet, pawing madly in the air. The blow of the hat upon his shoulder startles him and he makes a great leap forward, and another, and another, striving to plunge from under the terror that bestrides him. He takes an instant's counsel with himself. He cannot run from under the terror. He must dislodge him. Gathering himself together he leaps almost directly upward, coming down with stiffened limbs, humped back and all four feet together. Again and again, higher and higher he leaps. The force of his impact with the earth is terrible. The spectators lean forward breathless. Raley sees them through a blinding mist, every faculty of his being concentrated upon the one task of sticking to his steed. His young face is a furrowed mask of deadly determination. He gathers every last resource to meet some new emergency. What is it? The horse is shaking himself till his bones rattle in their sockets. Then, as if beside himself, he runs sideways, bursts through the slight inner railing that encloses the field, smashes up against the wall of the grandstand, and stands with head hanging, resource exhausted, confessedly beaten.

The marshal gives the signal. Time is up. The buckaroo has won! He leaps to the ground and bows to the wildly cheering crowd. And so, with the awarding of the prizes, the inlaid saddle to Joe Raley, youngest of the buckaroos, the jeweled bridle to the little lady with the bunch of curls, the chaps, the spurs, the lasso and the rest, so it closes—the great show, a show unsurpassed as an exhibit of native strength and physical prowess, not without brutality—a brutality that will pass away in the coming years before the finer chivalry that evolves the gentle man.

III

BUSINESS IS BUSINESS

On the fifth morning after my embarkation, I awoke in a gorgeously flowered bedroom (I still recall an uncanny effect of creeping things among the blossoms of that wall paper)—awoke to the five-o'clock clatter of stone china in the lower regions of my inn, to the aggressive cries of magpies on the near-by fields, and to the creaking of heavy wagons—two or three in a string and drawn by half a dozen shining mules—piled high with wheat for shipment. Athena is but a wheat-shipping station and, in this character, as the center of that wonderful landscape of golden fields and purple fallow rolling away in every direction, it fully compensated, to my mind, for its dingy hotel, its primitive little dwellings, and its unattractive streets. Autos came and went constantly between the wheat fields and the station. Continuous trains of wheat-laden wagons passed and passed. Marvelous Oregon fruit came daily to my lunch basket from eager little givers, and the tingling September days were enchanted days to me.

This is not a chronicle of pedagogical experience, but my brief term in Athena presents elements of universal experience that tempt me to include it. The Athena graded school was enjoying a revival, it would seem, from a state of comparative lethargy. The new epoch was marked by a renovated building, a new school board, a new principal, and a complete corps of new teachers. Several of the teachers had been engaged at the last moment, as had I myself, by telegraph.

A commercial department had been installed and my nearest neighbor in the hotel—a Kentucky girl—had been wired for, through an agency, to conduct it. Perhaps it was our proximity in our domicile that led her, in the course of the first few days, to confide in me a keen anxiety. The equipment for her department had been delayed, which made it impossible to open her classes the first week. This circumstance had blinded us all to any cause of wonderment that there were two commercial teachers in the force. Toward the close of the week, however, the principal informed her casually that she would not be needed. There had been an unfortunate error, he said, through which two teachers had been selected for the same place, and while they regretted any inconvenience to her, it was inevitable that they should let her go. To her alarmed protest, the principal replied that he thought there was to be a vacancy in the grades and that she might have that when it should occur. The salary would be sixty-five instead of eighty, for which she had been engaged, but it was fortunate that there was any opening at all.

The other teacher, who had been preferred, told her story frankly. A telegram offering the position to her had reached her home. Acceptance if proffered was to be immediate and by wire. She had been absent on a camping expedition and the telegram lay for some days unanswered. Upon receipt of it, she had wired that she would come on favorable reply and, receiving no reply, had packed up and come on the chance of being in time. The Athena principal, meanwhile, being informed by the telegraph operator that this young lady could not be reached, had immediately wired an offer of the position, stating salary and length of term, to the Kentucky girl, had received her acceptance, and considered the matter closed. The disturbing incident was the arrival of the first candidate.

The interval of delay in the furnishing of the department offered a convenient opportunity for gauging the situation. Probably the board and principal preferred the personality of the western girl—she was from Iowa—but I have always uncharitably believed that the fact that the rightful claimant was twice as far from home and male champions and gave, moreover, considerably less evidence of being able to fight her own battles was the determining factor. I gathered, from the southern girl's confidences, that there had been financial difficulty at home and that this venture of hers—a great venture for a southern girl—had been made in the hope of saving the day at a critical juncture. She was a thousand miles from home. She was already ninety dollars out of pocket. She had borrowed for the expense of her journey. She had had only commercial training, had never prepared herself for grade work, or had any experience therein.

In response to her solicitation I went with her to each member of the board—all of whom, as fate would have it, were lawyers. They admitted, severally, that she held a perfectly legal contract. She had preserved both telegrams—the detailed offer of the position and a copy of her own acceptance. They agreed to a board meeting, but would promise nothing further. The county superintendent was sympathetic, but curiously ineffective. A Pendleton lawyer consulted gave the opinion that there was no flaw in her case, but refrained from advising her to prosecute. In the end, penniless and weeping, she departed for a country school offered her, having indignantly refused the offer of grade work from employers who had already given her such a deal. Just here the curtain falls upon the affairs of my unfortunate friend and rises upon mine.

I was naturally considerably disturbed by my close knowledge of this small tragedy and my sense of justice was seriously outraged. On the morning of the girl's departure for a neighboring district, I visited each teacher and suggested that, as a body, we voice a protest against this unjust dismissal of one of our number and petition that her case be reconsidered. Previous to this time there had been the familiar murmurings—the dark looks visited upon one in authority when one of a band of employees is unjustly dealt with. It was a matter of grave surprise to me, therefore, that not one of the force was willing to connect her name and fate with the controversy. I was "in it" now. I could see that. Not only had I been associated with the discussion throughout, but now, to cap the climax, I had attempted to incite rebellion in the force—a heinous crime in the eyes of any "honorable board" and principal.

It was, therefore, in part a concession to fate, but still more a concession to my own emotions, that I sent in my resignation, asking that it be regarded as a protest against the decision of the board with regard to my friend. Immediately after writing this out I sent a full account of the affair to the state superintendent, through whose offices I had come into the Oregon school system. No notice was ever taken of this letter. When I learned, in the course of time, that my principal and county superintendent had been "whippers up" in the state superintendent's recent campaign and that our board members were active politicians I thought I had some additional light on the whole affair.

To my resignation, on the other hand, there was no lack of reaction. From that moment I was a criminal. Only one teacher—after having been summoned alone to the office and duly threatened—dared to sit upon my desk and swing her feet in full view of the entrance hall. Bless her! She was the youngest of the lot. The others studiously avoided me and hastened to disclaim all sympathy and connection with my activities. I had claimed the thirty days' grace allowed by law in which to place myself elsewhere, but was informed that my place would be occupied at once. Acting upon legal advice, I stood to my rights and returned to my schoolroom on the following Monday. The new teacher was in the building but did not show herself to me, and all that week I taught undisturbed. On Saturday morning the clerk of the board delivered in person an indictment of half a dozen charges involving prodigious offenses against the law which I had practiced during my two weeks of occupation, summoning me to make defense or accept dismissal. The bitterness of the document was antidoted for me by the fact that the principal had publicly expressed especial approbation and satisfaction in the opening of my régime, and also by a simultaneous offer by the county superintendent of a much more desirable position.

IV

THE NEW LAND IN AUTUMN

JUST one vivid picture of my second location as I knew it in late autumn, rises out of the obscurities of memory: The month is October, the region northeastern Oregon. The Pilgrim sits upon the projecting end of a slender footbridge that spans the big ditch that governs the new irrigation project in Umatilla County. The bridge is placed just where the ditch rounds the crest of a low, barren hill, and affords a fair prospect of the surrounding country. One can look far down the valley of the Umatilla on the right, and on the left can see the greater part of the extensive level tract that constitutes the Project.

The thoughts with which the Pilgrim surveys the scene lack animation. It is indeed a strangely colorless landscape—gray sky, gray hills, gray sagebrush tracts. Even the developing Project seems lost in the gray ocean of desolation. The little checker boards of fruit trees are leafless and scarcely visible. The fields are crossed at regular intervals by gray windrows of sagebrush, laid in the hope of "holding down the soil" till the crops shall spring.

The little homes are far away and blended with the dominant monotone. The Pilgrim's gaze drops to her shoes, which are white with volcanic ash through which she has struggled ankle-deep a long, long way. She is weary. Eastward, a gray-brown cloud is rolling up. It is one of the first of the season's dust storms. Westward, a similar storm of different origin approaches. A flock of sheep advance enveloped and hidden in an obscurity of their own creation.

There is a step on the footbridge. The Pilgrim arises startled. A black-robed priest is coming toward her—a figure as somber and colorless as all else, save for a pair of blue, black-lashed eyes that suggest he might once have played upon the Irish grass. He pauses beside the Pilgrim and stoically surveys the scene before them. "And how long have you been in this country, Madam?"

"One month."

"And how long do you intend to remain?"

"I came to locate."

"God help you!" and he resumes his walk.

From Stanfield—my location in Umatilla—I went down, during Thanksgiving week, to Baker, to attend the state teachers' association meeting. Here, while the usual lectures, methods classes, and exhortations proceeded, came the word of fate to me in the shape of a summons from my locator in Prineville, Crook County, Central Oregon, to come down at once to look at a homestead location just discovered that seemed particularly desirable. I ran the gauntlet of disapproving county superintendents and institute directors and finally secured parole and departed in great glee, not stealthily but nevertheless by night, for the land of promise.

Something was wrong with our schedule and I recall most distinctly being turned out at an unearthly hour in the morning at raw little Umatilla station, to procure the only breakfast that was to be ours. Here, while we drank warmed-over coffee, and made the best of bread and butter—with the cook in plain view frantically but hopelessly peeling raw potatoes—I had a delightful little word with Dr. Campbell, president of the state university. He, with Dr. Churchill, afterwards state superintendent, and one or two others of note had been speakers before the association and had raised my fallen estimate of the representatives in the state of the noble art of teaching.

Then came the Columbia and its sand dunes—the latter much more in evidence at that season than the river. I was later to see the Columbia in flood, filling the valleys, and affording the mightiest example of a river that I have known.

The Dalles was my changing point. At Baker I had been almost directly in line with my destination, but there is, even yet, no railroad across Central Oregon. One must go to this northern point—The

Dalles—and then almost directly south in order to reach that region that has a character and climate all its own. Near to the depot at The Dalles is a little building devoted to an exhibition of Oregon products. It is with amusement that I recall standing spellbound before a jar of Japanese persimmons—huge ones, they were new to me—and reading the label, "Royal Anne Cherries." Query: Was it an innocent error on the part of the labeler or was it an imposition upon the credulity of the tenderfoot?

All day we climbed the course of the Deschutes, a rapid, turbulent river walled by bare bluff mountains on either hand. Down through crevices in these mountains came, here and there, great flocks of "fleece" and fat cattle to the corrals beside the track, making, in their helpless docility, that pitiful appeal that some of us, at least, never escape. From the canyon of the Deschutes we emerged a little before sunset into a high, bare, flat country, where wheat had been. All around it purple mountains rose and, beyond, the wonderful Cascades glowed in the sunset light.

At Redmond I left the train. From Redmond to Prineville—twenty miles—in white moonlight—the auto stage carried the traveler over a strange, high, juniper-dotted, sage-covered flat, alive with jack rabbits, and it was late evening when we slid down the precipitous winding road from the table-land into the valley of the Crooked River, and saw the lights of Prineville in its wonderfully scenic location, carved from the heights about it, the streets marked by ranks of poplar plumes, planted by scme far-seeing settler of an earlier day.

Thanksgiving Day nineteen-eleven! It should appear in red letters in my chronicle—the day that I attained to El Dorado. Luminous it was, in fact, in Central Oregon—a glorious day. From frosty sunrise to frosty sunset, through all its brief but brilliant hours, I rode—now on bare Rim Rock heights, now in the deep-cut valley of the Crooked River, the lofty, mirage-like Cascades behind, before, that unknown quantity so long and vaguely imaged—my destined bit of the earth's crust, my freehold, my estate! My guide, the locator, was an interesting young engineer, enthusiastic, crammed with the facts I wanted, human and likable. We had a splendid day.

It was exclusively a live-stock country that we passed through. Herds of fat, white-faced cattle passed us, driven by scorched-looking riders. Great bands of sheep stirred dimly on distant slopes. In the river valley huge stacks of hay were already opened for the feeding season. Once a coyote stole out on a rocky promontory and watched us fearlessly. Ducks and geese rose from the river, jack rabbits jumped and jumped in the sagy borders of the road.

"Bonny View," announced my guide, as a group of big barns and stacks and a pleasant ranch-house loomed before us. "We will stop there. It is only five miles from your place." *My place!* I caught my breath audibly and he laughed. The Bonny View family were dining out, but we did justice to a hasty lunch set out for us by the caretaker, and then made all haste to reach our goal. Eagerly and nervously I watched the changing landscape. I had had a haunting fear that it would be tame. I knew what practical considerations would appeal to the locator. But it was not tame. The Maury Mountains, pine-clad and dignified, in the background, the abrupt, walled Rim Rock skirting the valley, the winding river with its alfalfa fields—but, "That butte," pointing with his whip, "that is Friar Butte. The land I want to show you lies at the base of Friar Butte." I loved Friar Butte at first sight. In the days to come, through the doubled and redoubled allowance to the homesteader, it was to become my own, almost entire, my upland pasture. Its shadow already lay across the deep wash land when we reached it—my fields to be.

The spring—the *sine qua non* of the homesteader—was frozen and not flowing, but signs indicated that it needed but a little deepening. It has, in fact, proved unfailing at a lower level. I felt no hesitation. It was predestined. It was mine. For the first time, with the butte and the Maury Mountains at my back, I stood beneath a cone-shaped juniper and looked across the still-luminous valley and the river to those other mountains that were for so long to feed my eyes with their changing colors of slaty-blue, rose-purple, and amethyst. This juniper, for its beauty, should be my dooryard tree, I decided. This view should name my place and the name should be Broadview—and so it was.

That evening there was a neighborhood gathering at Bonny View—an old-fashioned sort of country time that delighted my heart. It was a rare chance to meet my neighbors, thus happily and early. We played charades and ship comes in and tricks and then—wonder of wonders! where were we anyway?—in came huge dishes of cream ice cream and enormous slabs of layer cake. It was my first but not my last taste of the hospitality of Bonny View. The lady of Bonny View said to me that she longed to see the country settle up and that she had found much fault with my locator in the past for bringing so many bachelors to their neighborhood. "But if he brings as many old maids as old bachelors?" I ventured, without considering the implication of the remark. Everybody laughed at my naïveté, and I believe that from that moment dates the neighborhood choosing of bachelors for me. But alas and alack! You may lead a horse to water—they have never induced their bachelors to drink.

The thirty-mile return trip to Prineville the next day served to make indelible the first impressions of my country. That afternoon at the land office I took my first lesson in land description: "The southeast quarter and the south half of the northeast quarter and the lot one—Section Four, Township Seventeen, Range Nineteen East, Willamette Meridian." It was Greek to me, but on the map the little squares had more significance. I could almost locate my juniper tree. It impressed me greatly that, because of the curvature of the earth's surface, it was not one hundred and sixty acres that I filed upon, but one hundred and fifty-nine and some one-hundredths. My papers must go to the general land office at The Dalles and from there I should receive notice that my filing had been duly allowed, after which the land was mine in all essentials, except that it could not be sold or mortgaged until all requirements of residence and improvement should have been fulfilled and title won, three years hence.

V

THE NEW LAND IN SPRING

It was spring in Umatilla. The fragrance of the peach groves was a thing of the past, and little green spheres hung thick among the luxuriant foliage, but the air was heavy with the breath of sweet clover and alfalfa that billowed up to the very doors of the little homes of the Project and rolled across the thoroughfares, and stood knee-deep in the fields ready for the first harvest. Meadowlarks, prodigal of melody, flung their silvery challenge unceasingly skyward.

The Pilgrim heard her name called and came out upon the balcony of her boarding house. The teaching winter in the Project had passed swiftly and the day drew near for the beginning of her residence in Central Oregon.

"Put on your hat, Miss Andromeda. I want to take you to the Agriculturists' banquet. I want you to write it up for me. And, first, I'll take you a joy-ride to put you in the mood. Give you twenty minutes." (This to the Pilgrim's plea for time.)

It was the young newspaper editor, Yankee-born and college-bred, the evangelist of the Project, the indomitable prophet of good cheer, the intrepid booster.

Half an hour later, the Pilgrim tucked her summery skirts into the buggy and surveyed with tranquil satisfaction a perfect horse in the hands of a skillful driver. Rhythmically they sped out of the little settlement to the Project "belt," the horse's flying hoofs thudding upon the soft roadway that had so lately been fathomless ash.

"Now I'm going to take you clear 'round the Project," the young man explained, consulting his watch. "Our road is a horseshoe, you understand, the settlement at one end, the banquet at the other —twenty miles. Strictly speaking," he added, "we singly-blessed aren't in the festivities to-day, but they have to have us, you know, us advertisers. That's where we come in."

"There's Judge Gary," said the Pilgrim, as a sun-bronzed gentleman driving a light dray, piled with strawberry crates, emerged from the first homestead lane into the highway.

"Hello, Judge," hailed the young editor, pulling up. "How's crops?"

"One hundred dollars clear, off my patch last week," smiled the Judge. "Tell that to Mr. Croaker back East. Henry, take this to Miss Andromeda." A little boy slid out of the dray and came smiling to his teacher. "Part of them's from my patch," he explained.

"Look at those strawberries," cried the Pilgrim. "They're as big as eggs!"

"How would Homer describe them?" mused the Judge, feeling for a quotation.

"I don't know," answered the Pilgrim, "I don't want to think about Homer. I want to think about new things. It'll take a brand new epic poet to tell about the Project." Her companion winked at the Judge. "Convert, all right," he commented.

"Funny," smiled the Pilgrim, as they passed on. "A scholar like Judge Gary, and the most enthusiastic farmer of them all!"

"Takes brains to appreciate the situation. There are two of your pedagogues now." They had come abreast of a very new, unpainted house, on the porch of which two sober, middle-aged people were conducting a huge churn. They paused in their work for a brief greeting. "Don't forget our Decoration Day program, Mr. Bechtel," called the woman.

"Both taught for twenty-five years and then put all they had saved in here," said the Pilgrim.

"And a wise move, too," said Bechtel. "They're growing young."

"They are," she responded. "They've got the Project look. It's strange, that look; it's hope, I suppose."

"Yes, hope," said Bechtel, "a new beginning. 'No matter how barren the past may have been,' something like that. There's many a failure makes good in the new land, many a scapegrace becomes a respected citizen."

Homestead after homestead slipped past them—trim little bungalows, modern barns and henneries, blooded stock, rows and rows of beehives stocking up with the first alfalfa honey of the season, new orchards, tiny shade trees, promising a new land indeed for days to come.

"You see," explained Bechtel, "a project isn't just like any other new farming community. They're experienced people mostly, and people who have made good to some extent elsewhere. It takes money to begin on the Project, and the settlers invest carefully, good stock and all, you know. And taste! More taste in a project community than in any other of its size in the world. Hello, Doc! going to the banquet?"

A stout man, mopping a perspiring brow, came down to greet them at the fence. "Boosters on the road early," he remarked. "Early bird catches the worm, eh? Confound the banquet! Of course I'm going. But what about incubators, now? Two thousand eggs in, and temperature fluctuating these spring days till one can't predict anything. Gee! Young people," he exclaimed, looking out over the fields where a new alfalfa crop made green embroidery on the fresh soil, "if this don't beat sitting in a dingy office waiting for a measles epidemic! What do they do it for? What does *anybody* do it for? Get that egg ad in for me this week, Bechtel; I'm fairly snowed under with eggs, and that's a fact."

On their right now was a tract of sage brush as yet unreclaimed by the Project ditches. Even here spring rioted in blue flax flowers and exquisite pink daisies, and little, low-growing, unknown blossoms. Suddenly a man stood up behind the fence on their left—a man with the brow of a Shakespeare, an intense poetic face. He wore blue jeans and carried a hoe.

"Why, Dr. Graham," exclaimed the Pilgrim, "what are you doing?"

"Chasing the water, chasing the water. Little ditches will leak. But where bound? The banquet? I've a good mind to go along just as I am. What do you say, Miss Andromeda?"

"I wouldn't advise you," laughed the Pilgrim, "I'm afraid of Mrs. Graham."

But Dr. Graham proved another topic provocative of thought.

"A brilliant man from Union Seminary out here in overalls mending ditches!"

"And why not?" urged Bechtel warmly. "Is any one too good to work in the ground, and hasn't he just as good people to preach to on a Sunday as he'd find anywhere?"

"It's a wonderful little church—the only church I've ever known that was really union. Denominations, creeds even, don't seem to matter at all, and people are alive and wide-awake and interested."

"Close to life? No time to speculate on another world?"

"Maybe," said the Pilgrim.

Down at the far end of the horseshoe, at the hour of one, assembled a numerous company. The occasion was the fifth birthday of the opening of the Project. It was an ideal banquet-hall—the spacious barn, which served temporarily as a dwelling, while the future home rose slowly a stone's throw away. If, however, the housing was primitive, there was nothing crude about the waiting table that groaned beneath the finest products of the housewife's art. Fine damask, egg-shell china, cut glass, and burnished silver made a fit setting for the royal feast. All had brought heirlooms, for what more fitting than that the choicest relics of the old life should minister to this first celebration of the new?

They were both serious and gay, the merry-makers—a glad but responsible company, a peculiarly brainy and thoughtful rural gathering. Dr. Graham at the head, and the vigorous young school principal at the foot of the great table, opened and closed the festivities. The feast was, inevitably, long, and in order not to prolong it unduly, for restless custodians of calves and chickens, the toasts were given at intervals during the repast.

All stood for the invocation. The Pilgrim, looking up into the inspired face of the spiritual leader, thought suddenly of the blue jeans and the hoe. "Who shall ascend into the hill of the Lord or who shall stand in his holy place? He that hath clean hands and a pure heart." It was a word of hope he had for them—a word of hope and of confidence. Why *not* clean hands and a pure heart? Why not a clean community and a record both individual and communal that all the world might read? In this free and splendid country with its simple and wholesome occupations, why should they fall into sin and iniquity? "Be ye therefore perfect even as your Father which is in Heaven is perfect."

There was a toast to the housewives who had so bravely borne the burdens of the pioneer, and, from the housewives, a gay response to the breadwinners, who had turned the new soil and brought forth the first harvest. There was a toast to the business enterprise and prestige of the community. To this the young editor responded with terse and confident eloquence.

Judge Gary dwelt upon "Beginnings"—the mapping of a new community, the laying of thoroughfares to be trodden by generations yet unborn, and, less materially, the establishing of precedents, of customs and traditions, for which their children would call them to account for good or ill. Yet his word also was a word of hope. Not only had the

Project prospered beyond all expectations, but their church, their school, founded in unity and aspiration, their happy social customs, of which the present occasion was but typical—these things they might well be proud to hand down as an inheritance to their children. And, in closing, would not the loved schoolmaster, who had brought their children five years on their way, read again the poem with which he had honored the opening of the Project?

The New Land

So long has Nature ruled alone
  These desert spaces wild and still,
And fire and frost and wind and wave
  Wrought here the pleasure of their will;

While teeming life of land and sea
  In forms uncounted came and went,
Leaving a shell, a tooth, a horn,
  To show where æons they had spent;

Until to-day, millenniums long,
  The land is as we now behold—
These high, parched plains in blinding light,
  The sage brush gray, the rim rock bold;

And desert creatures each in place—
  The leaping jack, the coyote gay,
The sage rat, lizard, scorpion,
  The rattlesnake and bird of prey.

Then suddenly, across the Rim,
  Man comes one day with rod and chain,

The New Land in Spring

To ditch the desert, carve the road,
  And check the surface of the plain.

So here a moment yet it lies—
  A virgin land untenanted—
Where many mansions soon shall rise,
  Where soon a million feet shall tread.

And Nature chaste, expectant, fair,
  Awaits her lord who is to be.
Her little wards from bush and stone
  Peer out this being strange to see.

What are his loves, affections, hates?
  What is his war, his government,
His God, his Devil, what his rule
  O'er this new land, his tenement?

In this New Land no precedent,
  No binding usage, dogma, caste,
No stain of crime, no graft, no vice,
  No slavery to loom or last.

O Sunshine Country, what new light
  For darker lands may rise in thee!
What faith, what hope, what brotherhood,
  What new ideals of equity!

O youngest Land, so innocent,
  Some radiant angel take thy hand
And guide thee, for thy day has dawned.
  What shalt thou be, O fair New Land?

VI

INCUBATION

DURING my teaching winter on the Stanfield Project, my nearest associate among the teachers was a Dakota girl of Bohemian parentage. Her parents had been among those old-country adventurers who had risked everything on the American experiment and had made good. They had chosen as the first fruits of their good fortune the thorough education of their children. My friend's brother had cast his lot in the Hermiston Project only a few miles from Stanfield and she herself had bought a relinquishment there, on which she slept once a week during the teaching term. It became a custom for me to spend an occasional week-end with her there and to witness in the activities of the young couple—her brother and his wife—the weary and endless labors, the adaptations, the privations and hardships, the soaring hopes and the repressed despairs of the beginning homesteader.

It was through their generous sympathy with my own plans that I obtained, during my last month on the Project, the loan of an incubator and, at a marvelously low price, something over a hundred thoroughbred White Leghorn eggs. This was my very first step in an independent agricultural career and I took it with tremendous seriousness. Not only was it the first business venture, but I felt a deep maternal responsibility for the multitudinous little life entities that it lay in my power to kindle.

I am sure that my normal temperature became, for the classic three weeks' period, one hundred and three degrees. My testing incubator hand became as sensitive as the thermometer. Lacking the desirable basement for the machine, I became keenly aware of all weather changes, but regarded them as significant only as they tended to run the temperature up or down in that dark and dreamy chamber crowded with nascent existences. Daily I turned the white eggs with tender anticipation. I was reduced to despair when an egg dropped from my hand and a little live embryo floundered helplessly in the released albumen.

Unforgettable is that night of the cold snap when I woke from prolonged slumber and, anxiously seeking the incubator, found the mercury low in the nineties and steadily sinking. I put on all steam but still it fell. Frantically I built a fire and introduced pans of hot water above and below the eggs. The quicksilver was now out of sight. It is characteristic of an incubator thermometer to continue indefinitely in the direction in which it has got a start. After ages of waiting it appeared again. Very slowly and lingeringly it slid upward, and, some time in the next forenoon, stood once more at one hundred and three. I cherished small hope and my sky was darkened.

Next came that sudden heat wave. I had ventured on an excursion that took me several miles from home. Returned, I flew to the incubator. I annihilated the brightly burning flame. I stared stupidly at the thermometer. It didn't seem to register at all! Tardily I realized that the mercury was now out of sight—no telling how far—*above* one hundred ten! I was vanquished then, down and out? Still, I took out the tray of eggs and set it upon cool, wet towels. I laid cool, wet towels upon the eggs. Inwardly sobbing, I awaited the pleasure of Mercury, wishing that the whimsical onlooker would depart and allow me to bawl!

Still I pursued my hopeless round on the bare chance that, even after the chill and the cremation, some sparks of life might survive. On the evening of the nineteenth day, as I was performing my daily duty to the machine, I was arrested by a faint but vigorous hail. Bird, mouse, or cricket? I stayed my hand in wonder. Then, from directly beneath that hand, it came again—a chirp, this time piercing and insistent. An egg was "pipped"! The next morning, a weak and draggled pioneer had successfully arrived and lay weak and panting on the warm eggs. The whole chamber was alive with peeps and tappings. To my resuscitated hopes every egg was cracked. By night, the machine resembled nothing so much as a corn popper at its crisis. Brisk snappings, momentary evolutions, and first shrill cries of protest against the hardships of existence continued into the small hours. I oscillated feverishly between my couch and this cradle of a feathered brood.

On the final morning, the sun being well up and chill departed, I tremblingly approached the machine with carefully lined and padded basket. Stooping to turn the little buttons that hold the door, I became aware of three brand-new personalities, attired in softest cream-colored down, standing observantly together at the little round window at the front, and regarding me sagely with the brightest of black eyes. Within was a seething multitude, soft as thistle down, beautiful as flowers. I still trembled as I lifted to the new nest the spry and dry and fit, counting them meanwhile. A tardy minority must remain in the incubator for a little further maturing and polishing off. By night I had them all out—a three-fourths hatch, a contented, whispering, cuddling, exquisite possession. This my chilled and roasted brood—my forlorn hope!

VII

THE LIFE OF THE PIONEERS

PROBABLY as early as 1875 it had become a matter of knowledge to settlers on the border, that the high, dry plains and mountains of Central Oregon would maintain stock, and that, given sufficient area, the sparse bunch grass would furnish flesh as hard and firm as would the grass of the mid-west prairies. With the minimum of feeding in the winter season, the major portion of a herd would pull through from spring to spring. Of the minority who perished miserably in the late and early snows or in the drought of summer, since the survivors yielded a reasonable pecuniary profit, little account was taken. This is human if not humane.

Fully forty years ago, then, the covered wagon, containing a sufficiently complete equipment for one human family for an entire year, and a little "bunch" of stock—the nucleus of the herd-to-be—became a familiar spectacle in the streets of The Dalles, as they set forth upon a pilgrimage of from two to three hundred miles into the wilderness. Arrived at their destination, in the little valley of one of the infrequent streams, men and women side by side hewed logs and whip-sawed lumber for the new home, dug post-holes and erected fences and broke soil for the little crop of rye that was to be the winter's safeguard for the stock.

Women bore children apologetically in those days, because of the drawback to the all-engrossing work in hand, but bore them and raised them, too, for if it was a land without luxuries, it was also a land without disease. Children grew inevitably to stalwart maturity. They endured hardship, those pioneers, but still more did they endure privation, for the nearest market was distant two hundred miles and human calculation at the best is not infallible. Milk, butter, and eggs, somehow, somewhy, are always rare luxuries in a stock country, but to these people, upon occasion, flour, salt, sugar, and soap became superfluous. The stock throve, and, once a year, the man or men of the family group made the return trip to the railroad, taking a bunch of fattened steers and bringing back an ever-increasing supply of family comforts.

There were always neighbors, though far-distant. No one settled in the country quite out of touch with human kind. Perhaps a whole generation grew up guiltless of schoolroom vices, but in time came the log schoolhouse, and with it, the neighborhood gathering—the Christmas tree, the basket social, the dance, the candy pull, the picnic, and the "speaking." Anything beyond these even now belongs to the catalogue of those things of which the population have "never heerd," and savors of evil.

"Eats" in this land of large exertion and large appetites played the larger rôle. The basket social, from simple beginnings, evolved into a veritable Babylonian feast, contained in astounding funereal monuments of crêpe paper and paper flowers. Even at the present day, the tenderfoot who presumes to "charge for a program" without "eats" will reap the ignominy of the uninitiate. The gallant who will unhesitatingly produce a five dollar bill for an ornate and spicy basket will refuse fifty cents for a program. Wild horses will not drag it from him.

It was an unchurched population. Men brought with them denominational traditions, and occasional missionaries — Methodist, Baptist, Presbyterian, Disciples—stimulated the inevitable "wrastling" over predestination, baptism, the vices of cards and the dance, and the doctrine of sanctification. If one strolled in among them unprotected by one of the well-known brands of spiritual armor, he became at once "the *'in*-fi-*del,'* " and a mark for darts from every camp.

The moral law suffered liberal interpretation and was enforced by the ever-present firearm and the eye-for-eye and tooth-for-tooth acceptance. Drinking was almost universal, and drinking to excess not uncommon. Strays from the fold of chastity were many, and, having fed the fires of gossip for a brief season, were tolerated and their sins condoned. Extreme physical exertion at one season was offset by much inertia at another, and unusual or unseasonable effort was not to be thought of.

There were well-defined lines of neighborliness. There was always a place at the table and a quilt for the night for the transient. When desired, goods would be brought along the highway for the requesting neighbor, but and if this neighbor, through one misfortune or another, were unable to call for them, on the highway they would remain, were they the very necessities of life. Perhaps because of the strenuous independence forced upon each pioneer family, obligations of service to others came to be little recognized. The newcomer might remain indefinitely beneath the old settler's roof, but he might look far and long for help in erecting the new rooftree or in breaking the soil.

Toward other species than the human, principle and practice were hard and rigorous. Exploitation for human profit was the only recognized use of "the beasts that perish" and a naïve astonishment greeted any other viewpoint. Hunting and trapping were the pastimes of the winter season, and killing was the appropriate human reaction to the phenomena of animate existence.

VIII

"AND THE EVENING AND THE MORNING WERE THE FIRST DAY"

On the evening of the twentieth to the twenty-first of June, on the high, Central-Oregon plateau, there was well-nigh no intermission between twilights. White daylight faded out and sifted in again imperceptibly among the stars, and the longest day of the year began almost literally at midnight. Scattered over the vast sagebrush reaches, cattle awoke and stirred after brief dozing, nibbling at the tender bunch grass. Rabbits scarcely ceased their leaping from cover to cover. Coyotes mixed their vesper and matin rhapsodies, and the infrequent birds hovered their young for a brief hour or two and returned to the chase. East of the Crooked River, the bare, clear-cut mountain range grew slaty-blue against a golden sky. The air was crystalline in its purity. On the western side of the river and over against the mountain range, at the summit of a long slope of wash land and at the base of an aggressive butte, beneath the dense boughs of a cone-shaped juniper, a solitary human being had kept watch-night unwinkingly.

"Evening and Morning Were the First Day"

From beneath the incubus of civilization rises, every now and again, in the breast of one human being or another, the protesting spirit of the cave man. Even the cave woman, though at more infrequent intervals, asserts herself. Behold then, on this morning of the twenty-first of June, nineteen-twelve, one in the clutches of this obsessing demon of the cave woman—one whom the demon has driven forth, like King Nebuchadnezzar, from the haunts of men, to make her home with the beasts of the field, and to be wet with the dew of heaven till three times shall pass over. The Pilgrim, on this fateful morning, began her homestead residence.

At about five o'clock on the previous afternoon, the last faint rumble of the retreating wagon had fallen upon the Pilgrim's ear as something significant and epochal. Fifty miles to westward passed the nearest railroad line; one hundred and fifty miles to eastward the next nearest. Northward and southward the distance was so great as to be non-negotiable. On every hand, high, dry, and untamed, stretched the Central-Oregon plateau. Richly timbered mountains and deep river clefts made occasional dots and lines upon its vastness. No human habitation was in sight. Overhead, the dense foliage of a symmetrical juniper tree preserved a fresh coolness of shade from the brooding heat of the June day.

Under the Pilgrim's hand a shaggy brown dog,

absolutely relaxed, rested from the weary exertions of his long journey. Behind her her trunk stood on end and against it leaned a tent rolled and strapped. She had just opened a series of three splint baskets fastened on a rod, and now on every hand, leaping, running, flying, springing into the air to clap ecstatic wings, chirping a babel of wild delight, ninety balls of straw-colored down—potential White Leghorn fowls, just four days out of incubator—celebrated their freedom. Nine months before, the Pilgrim had stood in a palatial waiting room in New York City, buying her ticket for Portland. Now she was at home. One hundred and sixty acres lying about her were already entered in her name on Uncle Sam's records. Tent and trunk and downy flock were house and barn and blooded stock in embryo. "Chickens and wheat" she had decided when she staked the claim. Hence the now-liberated occupants of the three splint baskets.

On this first morning of homestead residence I had barely had time to wash my face at the spring and prepare my first cup of campfire coffee when two young bachelors, Grant Fadden and John Porter, arrived to stretch my tent. They brought a pail of warm milk. One of them was a beginning homesteader himself, and had a fellow feeling. They were exceedingly helpful in giving me my bearings and certain essential information that I should very soon require, as well as in setting up this my first shelter under the Central Oregon heavens. Everybody knew by phone that I had arrived and my first callers were not out of sight before others began to arrive. Three families of old residents—my near neighbors, into whose immemorial pasture my filings had intruded—paid their respects. It amuses me at this distance to picture what must have been the contrast between my unguarded and interrogative innocence and their shrewd reserve. What foundations were laid for future relations may easily be conjectured. One neighbor engaged offhand to break my first twenty acres "at the 'going' price" as soon as he should have broken a young horse for which he was about to go to the mountain. Another promised to haul the lumber for my tent house, since he must haul some for himself before threshing time and could make one job of it.

To inquiries regarding a more immediate need I obtained no response. All of my simple camp furnishings, including cot and chairs, were now at the post office four miles distant. Could my neighbors suggest how I might get them hauled? I did not allow my eyes to stray in the direction of the three teams tied in the offing. In response to this query my callers exchanged glances of puzzled consideration. They could think of no way in which the feat could be accomplished. Nothing could have been more typical of a certain phase of the "Old Oregonian" than these easy promises as to the future, this absolute unresponse as to the present. When my guests had withdrawn at the approach of dinner time, I stirred myself to gather juniper boughs for a temporary couch. On this couch I was destined to enjoy precarious slumber for one month, until at length a passing wagon, going to the mountain for wood, left my freight at my door.

Pilot Butte—a solitary, towering butte to the north of me—fulfilled the promise of its name in becoming my guide to the store and post office, three and a half miles distant as the crow flies. Within my first week was inaugurated that pilgrimage that, during the seasons following, made me familiar with every rise and fall, every tree and stone of the sage-brush tracts intervening between my tent and Uncle Sam's station. During that week also began my experience as a beast of burden. My carrying power came in time to be about forty pounds, and unlimited experiment proved the shoulders to be the normal resting place for a load that must be carried a goodly distance. Dawn, noonday, twilight, and white moonlight looked down upon these pilgrimages, and always beside the solitary human, with many a digression in pursuit of jack rabbits, frisked and twinkled and exulted the brown shadow, the inseparable companion, the dog of dogs. All summer I cooked on a campfire, for which I gathered rotting sagebrush and dead purshia, pleasing myself with the reflection that this was all in the way of clearing the fields where wheat was to wave the coming season.

Two nights at the very beginning of this summer's tenting were not without incident. On the third night of my residence, a brilliant moonlight night, my tent flaps having been left wide open to let the night air in, something waked me at about two o'clock. I lay for some moments with eyes closed, altogether unapprehensive. Then a loud thud close at hand startled both eyes and ears wide open. There in the white moonlight, directly in front of the tent, stood a saddled horse! Maybe I didn't know, after that, what it is to have a real chill and rising hair! I reached for my gun, which was close at hand and loaded, got it into position, and awaited developments. Well, hours went by while I lay there motionless. At length the horse deliberately moved away and I inadvertently fell asleep. In the morning the horse was feeding on the butte side, and toward noon his owner came for him, having lost him while following up some stock on foot the day before.

For several evenings after my arrival I had listened to distant sounds that seemed like nothing but the shouts of boys on a ball field. So many things were new that I did not concern myself unduly with this unexplained phenomenon. At an early date, however, soon after bedtime, there suddenly arose, as if from the very ground beneath me, such a chorus of howls and yelps that I sprang to my feet in panic. Bingo, to whom fear was always unknown, was in the thick of the powwow at once, but presently came racing back with a big coyote at his heels. Once on his own ground, he turned again and became the pursuer. And thus they had it back and forth till, in terror for fear he might be killed, I fired my gun into the air. Dead silence succeeded, but an hour later our visitor returned with reinforcements and, sitting out in the shadowy environs, proceeded to make night hideous and to challenge my infuriated but now enchained protector to come out and be devoured.

On one of these June mornings, as I sat under my juniper, came a rapid rider on a mettlesome horse. He proved to be John Porter and explained that his sister Mary, a homestead spinster like myself, had sent the horse with an invitation to spend the day with her. He himself was going to Ben Franklin's, just around the butte, to help out in the building of a barn. All of them were new settlers from the Middle West, he explained. They would be glad if they could be of service to me now and then. They knew the difficulties. (Little did I know from what pitfalls they would rescue me and in what crises they would redeem the promise.) Delighted, I left my little biddies with some misgiving and, letting out my eager horse, who wanted only an excuse to run home again at top speed, I came into Mary Porter's dooryard after a three-mile race with Bingo, like John Gilpin on his homing steed.

In a little hip-roofed shack, as neat as wax, Mary was paring potatoes from their spring-irrigated garden. This shack was her brother John's, she explained, and just around the bend of the hill, in an aspen grove, was hers. They slept beneath their own rooftrees, and ate now here, now there. Mary was full of kindly and helpful gossip about men and things. All is not gold that glitters, she reminded me, and one might well take one's time in choosing one's friends and placing one's trust. The bloom was already off the "Old Oregonian" for Mary. She was so sensible, so canny, I had a lovely day and another Gilpin-like ride home at sunset and a chat with John Porter returning from his building. I was interested in all of Mary's ingenious ways of managing in our primitive situation. She was most practical and wide-awake. She had one great advantage over me—a brother on the ground.

IX

WHITE LEGHORNS

AROUND my one hundred incubator chicks—the one materialized hope of my adventure—centered all the experiences of that first summer. From my journal I take a short essay on their engaging qualities:

"The little Leghorn has a brief infancy. At the age of two days the sprouting of the feathered wing is an accomplished fact, and, at two weeks, it has become a pearly shield covering the entire side—lustrous as a shell, exquisite in tint and curve. Elsewhere the straw-colored down persists, only gradually yielding to the coming plumage, till at six weeks the little head alone has the creamy hue, and at two months I have a flock of snow-white doves—for the Leghorn is in fact more bird than fowl, this early and excessive development of wing indicating special powers of aviation. Like the subject of the old hymn, the Leghorn 'would rather fly than go.' Watch a Leghorn hen take an eight-foot fence at standing flight or sail over a good portion of a block to reach a desired feeding ground.

"In considering the beauty of the little wings, one recalls that the progenitors of these chicks inhabited a land of art called Italy, and one wonders if, for certain cherubic appendages, Michael and Raphael and the rest may not have impressed a little flock of feathered models to serve at the point where the human infant lacked a limb.

"It is this light and flitting and birdlike quality that is, to me, one of the chief attractions of my flock, though I realize that to the fleshly eye that sees a chicken always in the shadow of the dinner pot, or in its extreme youth regards it as 'a little fry,' there are serious disqualifications. In fact one would not keep a Leghorn for a market fowl, although at six months, given a contented and well-fed youth, the result is a very delicate and sufficiently plump little body.

"Because of the temporary absence of my spacious farm buildings, and because of prowling coyotes, two of whom backed my valiant, brown defender to the very door of the tent one night, the chicks must be accommodated in a front corner of my tent.

"At about half past two in this latitude on these midsummer mornings, appears the first faint glimmering on the horizon. At about the same time comes the first premonitory chirp from my little dormitory. It is answered sleepily and there is perhaps a third.

"Number One, 'Isn't it morning?'

"Number Two, 'Is it? It isn't possible!'

"Number Three, to whom words suggest instant action, 'Let's see.' He pokes his head under the curtain. 'Yes, there is the morning star.'

"Numbers Four, Five and Six (sleepy heads from the rear corners), 'Sh-sh-sh!'

"That breath of air that followed Number Three's head into the dormitory was certainly chill. So everybody settles down for another nap.

"Twenty minutes pass. The horizon has become faintly golden. Objects have become dimly discernible; the breath of morning moves.

"Number One wakes suddenly and cries out, 'Why, did you go to sleep?'

"Number Two, 'Did you?'

"Number Three, 'It's surely morning now!' He creeps out from under the curtain. Others follow, slowly, cautiously, peering around, with stretched necks. (Chickens see poorly in dim light.) I can barely see them, like little shadow chicks, stealing about on the feeding ground in front of the tent, pecking tentatively here and there for seeds, seeking the water pan. This at least they can see. This little party is only the advance guard—thc hardy pioneers. Two thirds of the flock remain warmly content in the dormitory. In a moment back they come, more hurriedly than they went out, and cuddle ecstatically in the warm interior, with many a congratulatory expression: 'Oh, how good it feels!' 'Isn't it cosy?' 'How cold the ground was!'

"Another half hour. The east is golden orange, flaming, wonderful. The hills above it are clear-cut and slaty-blue. The thread of a moon hangs like a jewel in the high heaven. There is a sudden, tumultuous leaping to life in the dormitory, wide-awake shrill chirpings, jostlings. The curtain flies open before the turbulent throng. Out they come —jumping, flying, shrilly piping, leaping into the air, and madly clapping their birdlike wings. One division storms the fountain; another makes a rush for the sagebrush; the majority scatter over the feeding ground. In five minutes they are all gone— scattered over three or four acres—ferociously hunting the early worm, the sleeping grasshopper, the unwary beetle, and the sluggish fly.

"By eight o'clock, when my arduous daily labors are consummated, and I come out under the juniper with book or pen, they are a weary band of hunters, and return to perch about me in the juniper branches, to cuddle in the deep needle-bed, and above all, to drink and drink and drink again. They are delighted with the presence of Mother Hen, and vie with one another in securing the nearest branches, and in cuddling close about her skirts and feet—a twittering, sociable little company. One and another individual whom I begin to recognize jumps upon my knee, or places himself before me in a conspicuous attitude, hoping to be taken up.

"It is one of our stupidest traditions that feathered creatures lack susceptibility to affection, and are without intelligence. Truth is, if we have not obtained reaction here it is because we have not acted. The tenderest, most ethereal caress I have ever known was that of a ring-dove, and a petted fowl will lay its velvet cheek to yours with whispered phrases of endearment that can hardly be outdone.

"For a short season, rest beneath the juniper tree is profound. Then, suddenly, some leading spirit utters a shrill signal and takes wing. Instantly, the whole flock is up and away with a rush of wings, skimming over the sagebrush slopes like the white doves that they resemble.

"This program of alternate hunting and resting is carried on throughout the day, except that there is a prolonged rest, with only tentative sallies into the sunshine, during the heat of the early afternoon. At this hour, I bring out my rug, for it is already a long time since two-thirty in the morning. The brown dog digs his hollow in the juniper needles and settles himself with a deep-drawn sigh. And we sleep—the ninety-odd of us—long and deep, in the sweet freshness of juniper shade and high plateau.

"About four o'clock, a breeze springs up. The day is at once distinctly cooler. New life and impulses seize upon us, and we—the feathered ones—are off again, to wander far and long this time, till twilight drives us lingeringly home. And as in the morning we arose repeatedly, so at night, we must frequently retire between seven and eight-thirty, rising again and sallying forth with twittering flights and flutterings, only complete darkness finally determining our permanent occupation of the dormitory.

"One little fellow prowls alone, till, sudden terror of the falling night overtaking him, he flies shrieking into my hands, and cuddles there with gradually abating sobs, for all the world like a terrified child.

"For a long time there are chirpings in the dormitory:

" 'Do you remember that black beetle that was so hard to crack?'

" 'What about the green lizard that *I* caught?'

" 'You didn't hold him, though.'

" 'Bet you I will next time.'

"Sleepy-heads, 'sh-sh-sh!'

" 'What about the sour milk the neighbor brought us?'

" 'Fine!' 'Fine!' 'Fine!'

" 'Sh-sh-sh!'

"This is all until two-thirty, except pulling up the blankets one by one in the icy night, and hanging extra covers over the dormitory.

"On my fair and open hillside, in the white light of these days, the twin tragedies of life and death are infinitely enacted. Millions of tiny creatures rise out of oblivion, chirp, pipe, trill, squeak, rasp their brief note of jubilation, and pass, writhing and protesting, into oblivion again.

"The most minute victim of my downy and voracious horde is a tiny fly that haunts the sagebrush, and whose incubators I suppose to be the fruit-like growth upon the branches. The little fly swarms in the leaves, and the devouring host swarms in the branches, as contentedly picking and eating as children on a huckleberry excursion. Who knows what fateful devastation of the sagebrush may be thus averted?

"Huge anthills, knee-high, are objects of interest, but the ants do not commend themselves as food, and I doubt whether they can be eaten with impunity.

"The common locust leaves his shell in great numbers on the juniper bark, and creeps forth in fair maiden-armor, only to be seized by a foe hardly larger and much more tender than himself. Thereupon the enraged captive buzzes most terribly; the panic-stricken captor shrieks and rushes hither and yon, doing everything but release his prey. Eighty-nine chicks close in behind him, and the battle and the chase rage up and down and in and out, till, the original captor being overcome and robbed, or, the locust being reduced by mouthfuls snatched from either side, the buzzing and the skirmishing are gradually abated, and the whole troop retire for a much-needed rest.

"Field mice have hidden many a nest hereabout. In due time the pink, defenceless infants seek the light and fall victims in their turn to this new and unknown scourge that recently descended between the dawn and dark of a summer's day. A mouse is a dainty but difficult morsel. The hide is tough and cannot be broken. The approved method is to hammer the contents to a jelly and then elongate the body by successive attempted swallowings (each chick doing his part) till, after prodigious efforts, some well-grown and Samsonian individual lands it successfully at the goal. But woe unto him in whose throat it remains as a cork, for he shall presently be found stiff and lifeless, with a pink tail protruding from his bill.

"Little gray and blue lizards are much more tender, and the limbs may be dislocated and passed around. Tree toads and frogs are contraband, if, in migration, they should cross our high, dry field.

"Rattlesnakes are worthy of a complete line-up of forces—a fearsome, neck-stretching array, trilling their note of warning, till Mother Hen comes with the ax and performs the ceremony of decapitation. after which the body, having been slit open, becomes the occasion for a great barbecue and a powwow much prolonged.

"And when the neighbor-boy brings rabbits, a great bunch of them, furry little devastators of the fields—and Mother Hen skins them and hangs them about in the sagebrush, oh then the singing and the squawking, the gorging and rejoicing, and the gory, gory, plumage of the snowy flock!"

As in all Nature, so here, the preyer must be preyed upon. On the morning after my arrival in the new land, as I sat beneath the juniper, a graceful, red-brown bird, a little larger than a robin, with curved wings and hooked beak, alighted above my head. I drove him away (reluctantly) on the evidence of the hooked beak. Bird of ill-omen and precursor of much disaster! During this season and the following, I was to feed eighty plump thoroughbreds to him and his kind.

They came—the hawks—in greater and greater numbers, as the report of the happy hunting ground went forth—bird hawks and chicken hawks, perching hawks and soaring hawks, brown, black, and mottled hawks. They soared at all hours in the blue heavens above; they perched on the high butte side and spied upon us unwinkingly. They knew when I went to the spring; they knew the hours when I was busiest in the tent; they knew when I had not yet arisen; they knew—oh, scores of them knew—when I went to pay a call or to the post office. I grew sadly accustomed to the testimony of scattered white feathers and a little foot or two. Twicc I have seen a treasured pet carried skyward, while threats and chasing and hullabaloo proved unavailing. An old shotgun scared away untold numbers, but failed, in my hands, to bring them down. Only a change of location, at a later date, proved effective in lessening these depredations.

Just after the Leghorn chapter in my Journal, I find some notes on the general situation:

"And what of the *human* atom—a microscopic dot on the vastness of the wilderness? In the long, still days beneath the juniper comes the demon of the crystal desert. He squats before me and looks me in the eyes. 'Well,' he says, 'the days of a man's life are three score years and ten and you are getting on. What do you think of life on the whole? How have you made it—you and life? How do you intend to deal with him the second half? Who are you anyway? What are you in reality, away from all association and restraint? No precedents here, no dogma, no pride, no convention, nothing to live up to or down to now.'

" 'Smooth out those lines that were for other people—that smirk that was for Madam Blank, who held an exalted and erroneous opinion of your character; that seraphic smile that was for your zealous Christian Science friends; that furrow that was Professor What's-His-Name, interested in your mental processes; that humility that was generated in a Presbyterian cradle; that dignity that asserted and sought to sustain all sorts of things; that serene indifference that you visit upon your gentlemen friends. No good now to smirk or frown or pout. I see through you. Be a child again—a child of the desert. See, hear, feel, think, love, desire, believe! What is your religion—yours really? What are your opinions on the big themes? What inspires your spontaneous emotions? Who are you, anyway?'

"Sometimes he comes at night when I have pulled my cot out under the blazing stars. 'Well,' he says, 'what of the ideals that you confided to those stars twenty years ago? What have you done about them? Are they still yours? Are they workable?'

"At other times that old demon of agriculture, whom we all inherit, takes possession. He waves his hand and, lo, a golden wheat field where the sagebrush flourishes unchallenged. He points out my fertile garden and my alfalfa field, the little home I am to build, the lines of my fences, my pasture with its Jerseys and its Hamiltonians. He sets me to digging and hoeing at a furious rate, and to planning those larger operations that will call for men and teams.

"Inconveniences? Ah, perhaps. Thirty miles to nearest market; four miles to wayside store and post office. Uncle Sam having failed to furnish a horse with the homestead, all necessaries to be borne on back, *à la* the old woman of the mountains. All water to be carried one eighth of a mile up hill; all wood to be sought and chopped; all cooking to be done on camp fire in the midst of my harpy throng.

"I have crossed the Rubicon. On the thither side lie fifteen years of ardent schoolroom life, rows upon rows of little desks, the daily tension, the rigid schedule, principals amiable and crabbed, superintendents broadminded and arbitrary, school boards enlightened and ignorant, varying community requirements, social conservatisms, religious bigotries.

"For three years no binding contracts, no hours to keep, no patrons to please, no customs with which to conform, no conventionalities to respect, no standards to measure up to, no Mrs. Grundy to conciliate!

"Three years of one's own—infinite space in which to move, infinite freedom in which to think, to feel, to love, to act."

Do I look behind with wistful and vain regret? I withhold reply.

X

ACQUAINTANCE

This first summer on the homestead was, by comparison with those that followed, an idle summer. June, in that dry clime, is too late for garden operations and I lacked material for such edifices as I might have been working at. Trips to the store and post office, wood-getting, water-carrying, and my primitive housekeeping afforded plenty of exercise and I took many a trip of exploration among the buttes and the sagebrush fields.

My neighbors still promised to bring the lumber for my tent house, but the expedition was put off from week to week. A chicken house, however, I devised and, before the first frost, had the flock cosily stowed away. I made a dugout on the south side of the steep ridge that bordered my field, built up the walls with juniper trunks of which I cut more than fifty from the fields first to be cleared, roofed the whole with the same, and put a window in the front. A wired run, closed over the top, completed a hennery that, for the first time, afforded security in my absence. The dugout I would not now recommend. It was somewhat damp and I lay the first appearance of any form of disease in the flock to this winter housing.

I found much time for meditation beneath the juniper. Here I jotted down the first impressions of this new life, from which I draw from time to time in making up my narrative.

Acquaintances increased. On my second Sunday, as I sat beneath the juniper, busy with letters, two equestriennes crossed the sagebrush flat, drew up and dismounted, and introduced themselves as "The Nash Girls." Children of early settlers with ideals and energy, they live with brothers on the old homestead, though each of the large family has used his homestead right, linking together a series of valuable tracts which they administer together in the interest of stock-raising. A most comforting friendship had its inception on this Sunday afternoon. It marked the beginning of a thoughtful neighborliness without which I should hardly have weathered the blast.

Not many days later I climbed to the summit of Friar Butte and located a poplar grove which they had described to me. Taking my bearings from this, I slid down the precipitous thither side, made my way through or around ditched fields of knee-deep alfalfa, but not until I was within a stone's throw was I in any degree prepared for the oasis of the yard—a beautiful lawn, shaded by old poplars, and walled by a blazing defense of sweet peas. I almost cried out. I was already wonted to the dry and scanty growth of the sagebrush country. It was haying time and the first-cut fields were beautiful with dome-shaped cocks, the warm fragrance from which was almost overpowering.

The girls invested me with an apron and gave me a pan of green apples to prepare for sauce while they, quick and efficient, got ready the haying dinner. We had a jolly company at dinner and some good talk spiced with fun, for they are eminently a joking family. I mentioned my plan of experimenting with bees, and said that I believed that when the purshia ceased blooming they would get over the top of the butte to these alfalfa fields. At this the subject of current prices for bee pasture was gravely discussed—twelve cents per head a month said the oldest brother, to which I assented. This was the first of how many dinners gayly serious in the old homestead.

On Fourth of July morning I fired a sunrise gun, and, not so long afterwards, neighbors paused in passing to take me to the picnic. The picnic ground was six miles distant in a cleft of the Maury Mountains, in beautiful pine woods—the red-trunked, Rocky Mountain pine that took me back at once to my girlhood in the old Black Hills. Every one from my neighborhood was present, and even some of the "Basin" people from over the Rim-Rock, among these latter some firm friends-to-be, met here for the first time.

But such a spread! Such a country for "eats"! Beside all the hearty and substantial things that came forth from the baskets, there were strawberry shortcake with whipped cream—whipped on the picnic ground—loads of variously-flavored ice cream, "lovely" cakes with rich and mysterious fillings, and sweet and spicy preserves of many sorts.

I remember little beside the lunch and ring games in the afternoon. Did drop-the-handkerchief ever fail to break the ice of a new acquaintanceship? But I remember the sense of home when I got back to the tent and the little biddies, and sat for a bit in the moonlight with Bingo's head in my hands.

A paragraph from the Journal suggests the daily round of work and thought at this period:

"Sagebrush and purshia—a stocky evergreen shrub, decked out for a week or two in the spring with an exquisite, tiny yellow rose of compelling fragrance—encumber the soil and must be removed. In converting them into fuel, therefore, one serves a double purpose. For the quick fire both are excellent though unenduring.

"In this primitive existence one learns not to deplore the necessity for hard labor, but to find a daily wonder in the abundance of the first necessities of life—the brimful spring of icy and crystal water, the easily acquired and abundant firewood, the essential groceries brought three miles upon one's shoulders. It is when one is weary beyond words, hungry and athirst, that warmth and rest and food and drink yield, for the moment, the purest pleasure of existence. Through the absence of all conveniences, one learns from day to day what are the superfluities, and also what are the foundation stones of civilized existence. And in this simple life—the extreme opposite of coöperative industry—wherein one performs every necessary service for oneself, how one's heart goes out to the professional and perpetual toilers of the world—the hewers of wood and drawers of water, the plowmen and cooks and laundresses and scrubwomen who have borne our burdens upon their shoulders."

XI

THE BACHELORS

IF bachelors are, as reputed, unduly scarce in certain sections of our fair land, the fact is due to segregation. I reveal a secret that geographical exploration has laid bare to me. These bachelors, taken up by a whirlwind as it were, like snails out of a pond, from the region of the ancient community and the summer resort, have been rained down again upon the sagebrush tracts of Central Oregon. Here, philosophically transplanting themselves, they live their solitary lives, riding for cattle on grim Rim-Rock heights, raising their little store of hay, accumulating coin, and looking into a solitary future.

One by one, "upon their errands gliding," these bachelors passed within hail of the juniper tree, and paused to exchange the time of day. Occasionally the spell of the cool shade won them from their tenacious grip upon the saddle. Still more rarely did they come a-calling with malice aforethought. To the Pilgrim, their conversation was full of interest. It abounded in facts of the New Land—such facts as she was seeking—the soil, the seasons, the methods of the cattle men, the autumn chase for the scattered herds, the long, long trips to market behind the fattened steers, the short and arduous winter days when "feeding" consumes all the waking hours, the branding and the "turning out" on the tender plains of spring.

Gradually the Pilgrim's interests became interwoven with those of these earlier pioneers. She met them on gala days—at picnics, at haying time, at basket socials, at the rare church service. Walks and rides, on serious errands bent, occasionally coincided. A firmly-founded comradeship was gradually evolved—a frank and stimulating acquaintanceship.

The relationship of confirmed bachelors is like a second childhood. It is more concerned with the serious interests of life than with the personal relationship. The mind is freer than in youth for the enjoyment of active experience and interesting circumstance. Friends play and work together in greater freedom of thought and feeling. And, withal, there is a spice that childhood lacked—the spice of the fruit of knowledge, the consciousness of the complementariness of our severed nature. The very spiritual nicety of this happy state, its illusive and transcendent happiness, suggests that it is ephemeral and transitory. Who knows? Still, the joys we have possessed in spite of Fate are ours. "Not Heaven itself upon the past has power, but what has been has been and we have had our hour."

XII

THE OLD OREGONIAN

HAD I seen a band of white-faced yearlings, brand XYZ? I had. They had occupied my camp the day before, during my absence at the post office. Consequently I lacked the wherewithal for any species of bread stuff, ditto breakfast porridge, and was out sundry dishes and other perishable articles of furniture that had been trampled under foot. I stated the main facts, sparing details.

The Old Oregonian eyed me apprehensively. It was customary to retaliate for such depredations through the medium of a pitch fork, twenty-two shot, well-aimed bowlders, and broken plow points. I must have presented an innocent countenance, for he appeared relieved, removed his hat and wiped a steaming brow, and made an affable comment on the heat.

"Get down and cool off," I invited.

He dismounted with the stiff deliberation of the weathered rider, and sat beside me on the brown, juniper carpet. His hair was grizzled and his skin as swarthy as an Arab's.

"Power o' chickens!" (My little flock was skimming past in mad pursuit of a locust.) "All white. Rather have 'em mixed. Does better. Buy feed for 'em?"

"Have to buy wheat this first year."

"Won't pay. Won't lay for you before spring."

"Oh," I exclaimed, "the Leghorns lay at six months!"

"Claim so," said the Old Oregonian. "Don't believe it. Take it from me. Claim rye ain't good feed for 'em, either. My hens ain't never had nothing else—just rye 'round the stack. Kept hens for thirty year. Rye can't be beat for all purposes. Take it from me."

"And they lay in winter?"

"Lay in winter! Hens don't lay in winter. 'Tain't Nature. Takes newspaper city fellers to talk about winter eggs. Don't believe it. Raised hens for thirty year.

"Where's their mothers?" (This as the shining host repassed, led by the captured locust.)

"They're incubator chickens," I said—"hatched in a machine, you know."

The Old Oregonian's gaze was piercing and severe. I felt the power of his self-control.

"I'll show you," I said. I led him within the tent and exhibited the machine—the little drawers, the lamp, the water pipes. He made no comment whatever, but shook his head gloomily, and we resumed conversation only with difficulty, again beneath the juniper tree.

"How about the railroad talk, Mr. Hanson?" I asked.

"Railroad nothing!" he responded with vehemence. "Never seen one, never heerd one, never want to. Spoil the country. Spoiled every country they ever come to yet. Take it from me."

"Going to the Fair?" I ventured.

"Not me. Scheme o' them town sharps to git country money. That's all. Hog town, Prineville is."

XIII

THE QUEST OF DIOGENES

I HAD engaged to teach the little school of the district this first season, the date of opening being set for September first. My arrangements for lumber having been made in June, I had counted upon being cosily housed before my daily work began. Only the week before this date, however, I discovered that my neighbors had made their trip to the mill, had decided to bring a full load for themselves, and did not wish to make another trip. Frost came early that year. Hard ice had formed a time or two and it was already a little more than cool in the open tent.

Equally ephemeral proved my plans for breaking. I had laid very careful plans. I had one hundred dollars for putting in my first crop. No need immediate or distant was permitted to infringe upon this sacred store. The neighbors who had agreed to put it in were expansive upon the subject. Many a quarter-hour during the summer did we put in discussing methods. They were interested in seeing me get on, they told me. They could do the work for me economically and save me expense at the outset. Ah well! October found me diligently advertising for man and teams. My seed, laid in two months before, occupied a goodly proportion of my tent shelter.

The first and rather surprising fact brought out by the advertising was that our neighborhood had no citizens who needed to work. Beyond casual inquiries as to my success in securing a hand and what seemed to my puzzled understanding a certain secret satisfaction in my negative responses, no interest was manifested in my agricultural plans. As a tentative explanation of this early experience I register a remark of the Old Oregonian's with which I became familiar at a later date: "The only way to deal with them homesteaders is to starve 'em out. Take it from me."

However, on a certain notable morning in late October appeared beneath the juniper tree a charitable near neighbor. He was an Old Oregonian by marriage only, town-mannered, assured of speech, benevolent of mien. He, as a neighbor, was concerned about the Pilgrim's crop. He wished to see her succeed. If he could but see his way clear, he would himself, even at considerable sacrifice, undertake the breaking of her first twenty acres. The price offered (arrived at through the most diligent inquiry as to the usual thing) was of course something of a joke. As a business proposition he would not give it a thought, but for a woman's interest, etc., etc., etc.

Humble and grateful questioning on the part of the Pilgrim induced him to meditate deeply. Under certain circumstances there was a bare possibility that he might undertake it for her. Further eager questioning elicited the facts that he lacked certain essential machinery for the work and would need an extra team which was just now for sale. In order to provide himself with this equipment so as to get the crop in at a safe date, he would have to have an advance of fifty dollars. In fact, and after careful thought, if she were thus prepared, he would close with her on the spot. Some vestigial trait of shrewdness awoke and prompted the elated Pilgrim to bring forth pen and paper and take receipt for fifty dollars with details of the contract. The work was to be complete by November fifteenth. The man had a friend who would use one of the teams. The Samaritan thereupon departed with the air of one conferring a colossal boon and the Pilgrim relapsed into a dream of her golden harvest with white hens straying through its rustling stems.

There are periods in every life history upon which it is well not to dwell at length—experiences that sadden even in retrospect—the death of buoyant hope, patient anxiety deepening into despair, doubt supplanting confidence, gratitude metamorphosed into resentment. The sequel of this transaction?

On a soft April evening the Pilgrim received a legal envelope containing her fifty dollars, less the ten per cent lawyer's fee. The sagebrush slopes were still unbroken. The first harvest would be one year late.

XIV

DINNER IN THE BASIN

THESE are my vivid memories of one typical social event of this first autumn:

Hay harvest is long past and the untouched stacks augur well for the "feeding" season. The threshing machine with its invading army has scourged the land and left still a few measures of grain in the bins. "Riding for stock" has not yet begun, for pasture is good this year and cattle will remain long on the ranges. Fall plowing of the hay fields is now on, but this is only October and there is no haste. So, in this little lull of the year's labors, in this bright time before the lowering of the long winter, there is to be a "little dinner" in the Basin—one of those little dinners that are becoming quite the thing with a happy circle of us—friendly gatherings that make a strong appeal to the new and lonesome homesteader.

Retiring early last night to be ready for to-day, I saw, between the curtains of my tent, a huge, orange globe slide up the cool and slaty east. This morning, simultaneously with my own rising, a blood-orange sun timed itself almost to the moon's setting.

Dinner in the Basin

There is a tang and a tingle and a thrill in the air as of joyous things about to be. Biddies are fed and tent in order, and I am only just settling my white cotton tie when next-door-neighbor-homesteader Ben Franklin, in impeccable attire, appears with the horse I have chartered—a fleet, long-limbed cow pony whom I dearly love to ride. Ben Franklin is a lovable boy from Chicago, seeking his fortune in this far land.

So we two set out—the first of a numerous company—and gather a following as we advance. Descending from his mountain height, Andrew DeLong—a stately, dark-browed native of the soil, with a reminiscence of Indian in his eye and hair—is our first recruit. Next we pause at the open door of a little shack and salute Mary Porter and her brother. Mary is teaching now beyond the mountain, and rides home each Friday evening to sleep two nights on the claim and to establish Yankee system and order in her brother's neglected bachelor abode. Mary has a bright greeting for each of us with the exception of Andrew, toward whom she assumes a rather haughty bearing, yet with whom, nevertheless, she presently falls behind, and is not heard from more till dinner is half over. Ah, well do I foresee—but enough. At the Nash ranch—one of the flower of the old-time ranches—we acquire the three girls. They come racing down to meet us, straight and agile on their sprightly ponies.

The brothers are "riding for stock" in the Basin and will join us at dinner.

We pass a ranch house here and there from which we get no delegate, and only an indifferent or defiant greeting. We are the interlopers who have cut up and fenced the ranges, and brought in the new day—the day of the small ranch and more intensive farming, succeeding that of unlimited range and a minimum of labor. There are feuds, moreover, among the old-time residents—relics of sheep and cattle wars and lawless acts visited by neighbor upon neighbor. Those who join us not, perchance, run not with those who do.

The Rim-Rock is the name given to what remains of the cap rock of the region, topping high ranges here and there—a lofty table land level as a floor, the summer feeding ground of stock. Our way lies over the Rim-Rock, a long and arduous climb, and down on the thither side into a favored and fertile valley known as the Basin—somewhat inaccessible, and innocent as yet of the toot of motors or even of the threshing machine. We climb deliberately, pausing now and then on level terraces to breathe our steeds, and to enjoy the expanding view of valley and mountain. Even on these high slopes, little homestead shacks and broken acres testify to the rapid populating of the country. Here, at a turn of the road, a grave and modest young horseman awaits us, chary of speech but quick in response, with a sweet smile and snappy eye. Son of an illustrious New England family, near relative of a famous New York preacher, he is bravely hewing out his way alone in the Land of Promise.

We are a cheerful crowd and a friendly as we ride and chat, comparing experiences of other days and scenes, or consulting over problems that are similar and immediate. There is a fresh, free comradeship of the homesteaders—a hopeful, hard-working, out-of-door sympathy—that comes near being an ideal camaraderie of men and women. Hard-working bachelors we are, with human sympathies and understandings.

On the top of the Rim-Rock—merely a narrow ridge where the trail crosses—we cry out at the wonder and the beauty of the low-lying valleys on either hand, and we hang like eagles above them both. The autumn air is sparkling and delicious. Sagebrush is in bloom, and in fertile dimples of the slopes waves its yellowish brushes with their spicy odor. Yet it is a bare, bare landscape that we look upon—bare and gray. Pines on the mountain tops, junipers dotted over the lower country, and rare little patches of golden aspens hugging the springs—these constitute the forest features. No jungle or shrubbery, no vines, no soft obscuring undergrowth. Bare, bold mountains, bare plains, and gray sage reach to the landscape's rim. The second half of our journey offers some level stretches on which we may do some speeding, and we avail ourselves of the opportunity, for the climb has taken much time and the October days are short.

The ranch of our destination lies near the center of the Basin—the home of one of those rare old-time families whose large hearts and sympathies have welcomed the new age and the new comer. Huge haystacks dwarf the barns into insignificance and we know what a multitude of white-faced cattle will come presently down from the Rim-Rock to winter here. Careful irrigation has made possible a fruitful orchard and an acre of small fruits, also shade trees and a lawn. Neighbor women are helping in the kitchen and men stand about in the stack yard, ready to take our horses and to give them the fat of the land. We gratefully stretch our stiffened limbs and seek the warm and fragrant kitchen and the hearty welcome that awaits us.

On a long table built for the occasion, our dinner is already being spread, and we sit down without delay and without formality—the shy bachelors segregating themselves and those more gallant seeking places beside the far-outnumbered feminine elements of the company. Turkey, smothered in dressing and drowned in gravy, head cheese and sausages, mashed potato beaten light with cream, delicately canned string beans, onions, carrots, and turnips expertly served, cold slaw with whipped cream, creamy Dutch cheeses, deviled eggs, brown bread and white bread and tender "sour dough" biscuit hot from the oven, golden butter, steaming coffee and pitchers of buttery cream, marmalade, jelly, preserves, sweet pickles and sour pickles, fruit pies and cream pies, canned fruits and various cakes, and always cream and cream and cream. This is the "little dinner" to which we are so modestly bidden.

This is the luxury to which the sweat of the brow and the hopeful heart have attained in the New Land.

The talk is intermittent—appetites being so keen, and satisfaction for them so abundant. Such as there is is jolly and facetious, and we are better friends for having sat about this board in company. The sun is low and frost is already threatening in the shadows when we speed our way homeward—up to the Rim-Rock summit and precipitately down again.

XV

"BEHOLD, IN THE TENT"

In spite of constant anxiety as to crop and domicile, my early walks to school through the tingling autumn air brought elation and unflagging optimism. I did the seven miles daily without a thought of weariness. Certain conditions attending the opening of the school were as typical as were my industrial adventures. It happened that the chairman of the school board that year, though of pioneer family, enjoyed, together with his wife who had been a town girl, the reputation of being "high-toned." He had large business interests and their ideals of living were more refined than those of their neighbors. Hence, though they were exceptionally well-qualified to lead in neighborhood affairs, anything that they started was doomed at the outset.

The chairman having desired to open school on September first, it behooved the Old Oregonians to frustrate the plan. Having been unsuccessful in changing the date, they decided upon a camping expedition to the mountains and removed from the neighborhood for the first month three fourths of the pupils—the total neighborhood quota being four boys. Throughout September I taught one quiet and lonely little pupil, comparing the experience as to wear and tear of nerves with one in which I had conducted eighty pupils, with the help of an assistant. About the first of October the other boys came into school and I began my study of Old Oregonian boyhood. These boys were all natives of Central Oregon. Prineville—thirty miles distant—marked their most daring adventure into the world. They were bright naturally, but little drawn out mentally, and they were already somewhat bound and blinded by the prevailing bigotry. Anything that was "different" was condemned without a hearing. They had the habit of ridicule of all foreigners and foreign ways. However, we got on very well as long as I confined our activities to the schoolroom.

As the days grew short, I had barely time, after reaching home, to get in the night's allowance of dead wood, to feed the chickens and give them a half hour's freedom, and to bring water for myself and them. I shall never forget how each evening as I mounted the last ridge on my homeward way, I looked for men and teams in my sagebrush. It was a will-o'-the-wisp that led me many a weary chase before I caught it. On Hallowe'en evening, however, I spied from afar something new and glistening within my boundaries. John Porter had dropped his own work for a day and brought the lumber for my tent house. Fortunately it was not "dark of the moon," so, during the next week, in the cold and brilliant moonlight, I set up my little tent house and moved in on the second Saturday, having roped in a passing stranger to help me raise the tent pole.

From the Journal I take a few notes as to my tent-dwelling days:

"The dweller in tents becomes an expert in meteorology and a student of distant spheres. It was inevitable that the nomads should be students and worshippers of the heavens. If one is a light sleeper there is no change by night or day but becomes apparent. Changes of temperature, of humidity, of air currents; precipitation, whether rain or snow or sleet or hail; the clear or cloudy sky; the phase of the moon; the areas of the horizon traversed annually by the rising or setting sun; the ascendant planets; the shifting constellations.

"Living so close to Nature in seemingly so frail a tenement breeds confidence in Nature's self-restraint as well as in the adequacy of the well-set tent house. When the cloudburst finds you, as find you it will sooner or later in Central Oregon, you stand beneath your ridge pole enjoying a filtered downpour that drenches every exposed article in your habitation. But when there falls a bombarding and unmerciful visitation of hail that, perchance, beats holes in the shingled roofs of your neighbors, it bounds harmless from the yielding tent. When the furious semi-tornado from the southwest which is due five or six times in the course of the year has you in its clutches, you cower and hold your breath, your house is shaken like a rat. Books, dishes, jars of preserves, fly about your head like tokens from the spirit world. Yet, when the fury of the storm is spent, the dwelling is intact. The roof that bellied like a bubble about to burst resumes its former shape—through yielding has come off conquerer—while so-called firmer structures may be leveled with the ground. In dead of winter, it is difficult to find a cosier habitation than a well-built tent house, furnished with a vigorous little heater and a pile of juniper wood. In the heat of summer it is uninhabitable, but the owner turns out at this season to labor in the fields, and night finds it cool and sweet for well-earned rest."

And while hopes and temperature rose and fell during these autumn days, came the inevitable marketing incident in the Leghorn flock. Chickens for eggs had been my sole purpose from the first, but there comes a day when the superfluous little cocks must leave the flock. When I awoke one glorious autumn morning and heard my little chanticleers calling up the sun for the last time I suffered an acute pang. John Porter had agreed to come at twilight after the victims had gone to roost. I saw to my ax that it should do its part and I steeled myself to hold each victim, in order that no terror or bungling should darken these last moments and my memory. So quiet was the operation that each little cock slept with head under wing till his turn came. At last, sick and weak, I viewed the snow-white pile and dismissed John Porter with his price and with my lasting gratitude. He had been very quick and sure.

All day Saturday and all day Sunday I scalded and picked and the cold pile of white plump bodies grew and grew. On Monday of Thanksgiving week, which was vacation, I went to town with Ben Franklin and John Porter to peddle my wares. It was a new experience and an interesting one to seek the back door and offer country produce. How nice the women were! Everywhere I had a little chat and not once was a chicken refused. They were attractive chickens and it was Thanksgiving time and chickens were scarce in town. Prices were good and when I returned it was with a fat little purse—the very first returns from Broadview. And at about this same time, the little pullets came to the fore with bristling red combs and frantically cawing demeanor. A new era was begun and I provided a worthy basket, since collecting eggs from a true Leghorn flock is no mere form. The Leghorn hen is born to lay, and one must have a market ready, else one will be snowed under and entombed in the accumulating product. Lovely, white, red-topped biddies—ever cheerily singing, tirelessly active!

During this fall came Kitty Kat to Broadview—gift of Aunt Polly Fadden, whom I shall have occasion to mention more at length. Kitty Kat was a two-months'-old kitten, silky black with snowy trimmings—she was born most exquisitely neat. Bingo accepted her tolerantly, though not desiring her, and she became at once a *sine qua non* of family completeness. One who has failed to test the winningness of a young cat has not come into the whole of his inheritance.

Shortly before Christmas came the basket social. I attended with a simple white box decorated with decalcomanie and containing the best of my culinary art so far as the limitations of my situation permitted. I was to receive a stunning blow. The whole front of the room was banked with crepe paper edifices Ionic, Doric, Gothic, embellished with such paper wreaths and blossoms as no clime had produced for me. These triumphs were auctioned one by one by the wit of the neighborhood and brought in some cases huge prices by the very arrogance of their bearing. My own shamefaced creation was bought cheap by an itinerant stranger, who had truly the appearance of the wild man of Borneo. Tremblingly I shared fried chicken and sponge cake with him, expecting every minute to see a boomerang projecting from the folds of his garments or to see him run amok through the splendors of the spread. Being truly a trifle apprehensive lest he might think his obligations included walking home with me, I slipped out early and made tall tracks for Broadview. I had gone only a short distance before I heard steps behind me. I increased my speed, but so did my pursuer. Unable to keep my distance, I faced about, ready for my last fight, and met Ben Franklin's laugh. We were coming to be good friends, as young brother and big sister, and Ben had fully appreciated my position. We had a lovely moonlight walk in the crisp frost, during which my ignominious failure and my wild *tête-à-tête* became altogether delightful and worth while.

My Journal commenting upon this incident confesses briefly:

"What sort of old maid am I anyway that I can't walk home in the moonlight with an attractive boy without tingling from head to foot! Good reason why devoted hermits segregate themselves. In the peace of Broadview I haven't felt this way for lo these many moons."

Winter came on apace and the first week of January was a test of the pioneer. Parents requested that school be closed for a week, and I spent it solitary, as my Journal notes:

"We have had a little touch of 'dead-o'-winter,' with deep snow. Rather than break a trail while the storms continued, I have remained at home and rather closely in the tent house with the exception of the hours required for stocking up with wood from my piles one quarter mile distant—a serious offset to the relief from the regular seven-mile walk through the snow. I have done much reading, writing, mending, thinking, but rather dully, for the gloom and cold oppress me somewhat. The sun, appearing, if appearing at all, in the mid-forenoon and disappearing only three or four hours later, seems a negligible influence in dispelling the cold and frost. I see this is the phase just opposite to those endless and cloudless days of June. I have viewed with some concern the exhaustion of my stock of matches, but my fire has, for some time past, kept invariably through the night, and I have trusted to a continuance of the practice.

"This morning I awoke to a zero temperature, a sleety wind beating upon and through my little shelter, and a sparkless stove. I was due again in the schoolroom to-day. I dressed as quickly as possible, pausing frequently to warm stiff fingers within my clothing that I might be able to cope with the absolutely essential pins and buckles. I fed and watered the chickens, since I expected to be gone all day, and started on my customary walk to business—three and a half miles through unbroken drifts. I had had only a frozen biscuit for inward cheer and I was in acute pain at the start with fingers and toes.

Well, I wallowed and skidded and tumbled and wept like a complaining child. I record this hour of comparative torture since it was very real, but it is easily forgotten. No one came to school, so I walked on to the post office, where I was generously warmed and fed at an always hospitable table."

One more event of this first winter I must chronicle since it left me a sadder and wiser pedagogue:

It seemed to me that the obligation rested upon the school to present some form of neighborhood entertainment in the course of the year, and beside this I wanted to increase the library. Our chairman's family took great interest in the plan and so also did the little group of newer residents who had been my special friends, so also the Nashes and others of the broader mind among old residents. There was in this group considerable talent of various kinds and I very quickly located and had promised sufficient numbers to make a good program. We invited in addition all of whom we could learn who had formerly performed in public—histrionically, musically, or otherwise.

We held a rehearsal a week before the intended event. Not one of those whom we had learned to call the obstructionists was present, and we had reports from all sides as to the reaction to our plan. Charging for a program was an unheard of and preposterous thing. If we had had "perfessionals" to offer it might do. And only cake and coffee for "eats"! Fifty cents should call for ice cream at the very least. And then those books. Wouldn't anybody rather have a book of his own than buy one for the schoolhouse and buy the one he wanted, too! The books desired it appeared were of a very doubtful nature and likely to be corrupting. The whole thing "stuck in the Old Oregonian's craw," which was sufficient. It appeared that they meant to boycott the thing in no uncertain manner. In this predicament, the chairman's wife invited the company to give their program at her house, which we did, spending a very delightful evening, not without the coveted ice cream but quite without an entrance fee and with no results to the library.

Before leaving this school year, which was in spite of all a pleasant and friendly year in the schoolroom, I must record a crime of my own which is probably known at this date in every district in the county. Not one of the one hundred and sixty school pilgrimages of the term but Bingo shared. He was dignified and unobjectionable in the schoolroom, lying always at my feet except when he would occasionally stretch himself and ask to go abroad. It is reported, however—an "echo that rolls from soul to soul and rolls forever and forever"—that on one fateful day I allowed Bingo to drink out of the school water bucket. What foundation this legend has in fact I have never been able to determine. My record is soiled with many a similar eccentricity, and I know many a clean and healthy beast that I prefer to drink after rather than after many a human. In their anxiety after what was hygienic and sanitary it had never appealed to the district to provide anything more advanced than an open pail and a cup or two. Into this pail was dipped the cup of any casual tramp, for we were on the thoroughfare that crossed Central Oregon, two hundred miles long. Into this pail went also the common cup to refresh a seemingly consumptive member of a school family. This, however, never aroused comment. It is on the books that a beast is unclean and unclean he must be.

XVI

SPRING

By the time the school term was closed I had one hundred and fifty eggs ready, and in the freedom of that final Friday evening I fired up the incubator and inaugurated the season's work. From then until fall I was not without chicks of all ages—beautiful little herds that must be regularly fed from five to three times a day, watered at all hours (carry water for five hundred and learn their amazing capacity), watched unwinkingly, sheltered from wind and changes, and tucked up with careful judgment at bedtime, not to mention unfailing nightly excursions to see if all is well at two o'clock in the morning, when all the heat of the day has escaped from the earth's crust through the crystalline atmosphere of the desert.

With the close of school, too, came friends from the Basin to do my first breaking. They would not see me cropless a second year. They were homesteaders themselves and had had troubles of their own. They tented close by and day by day I walked out to see the new sod curl from the plow and the sagebrush piles rise high and higher. Now and then at twilight we burned the piles. Sagebrush has a way of its own when it comes to burning. It rises in a wonderful, clear flame and breathes incense upon all beholders.

The garden site had long been chosen, where grass grew in unbroken luxuriance and the gentlest of slopes promised both drainage and easy tillage, and where the sun lay longest through those endless summer days—for the season is short and there is no sunshine to spare. I cultivated an acre by hand that summer, doing everything except the first breaking. The Journal tells it with something of the immediate warmth of the experience:

"While the soil yet rests in frozen somnolence, the seed catalogue with its alluring cuts, its suggestion of all fruitfulness, claims many an evening. We check and recheck our careful list; we order while the snow yet lies white upon our fields, hoping to cajole and coax the tardy spring. Our little packages of varied shapes and sizes fascinate us like a miner's hoard. There is a new thrill in the spring breezes and in the loosened waters. And when, after the thawing and the drying, the soil is at last ready for our tools, what glad though back-breaking days are ours, turning and hoeing and raking to a perfection of granulated fineness. Our bodies at night are an incubus of exquisite weariness and small aches in unaccustomed places. We feel a new joy in the evening's peace and in our little circle gathered about the door-stone, be it only the faithful domestic companions of the solitary homesteader. Later, in luxurious relaxation, we resolve to write an ode to the immemorial couch, and we know nothing more till golden dawn and the song of robins bring glad memories of the task in hand.

"What queer little things seeds are, and how various the taste of plants in styles of swaddling clothes! How similar the parsnip and the radish in manner of growth, yet what more unlike than the compact and polished little sphere of the radish seed and the winged and airy potential parsnip. How we love to let them slide through the fingers and with what tender solicitude we rake the warm earth over and pat it down! Beans and peas are so immediately suggestive of the gathered harvest that we drop them with trembling fingers.

"Thereafter sun and shower are in peculiar measure our own. We seem to be sympathetically swelling and basking in the beneficence of Nature. It is wonderful to see little lines of green appear just as we designed them. We had hardly expected that. The delicate tracery upon the black soil is our own pattern—a living embroidery growing daily in relief and beauty. Hoeing is a joy, notwithstanding that the weary limbs must be stretched many a time beneath a friendly tree in sheer inability to labor farther. And, when the season of hoeing is over for the time being, we understand for the first time that familiar phrase 'laid by.' The crops are 'laid by'—consigned to the mercies of sun and shower, free to fulfil the instinct of growth whereby each plant attains to its 'peculiar difference.' We have done our part. The rest is 'up to God.'

"Did we really raise those crispy, crimson radishes, that early lettuce? What more delicate lunch combined with delicate white eggs from the Leghorn flock? Are those fat peas ours, dropping like little beneficent bullets from our fingers to the pan? The tender red beets and early turnips; the unending 'messes' of waxy beans! We have never cared greatly for summer vegetables. How have we suddenly become a fanatical devotee? And in carrying cool, green offerings to the neighbors, we feel that we are sharing a princely portion. In spite of your towering cities, your bewildering and multitudinous metamorphoses of Nature, still, 'while the earth remaineth, seedtime and harvest shall not cease.' "

Sometimes as I hoed, or shepherded my white flocks, John or Mary Porter would come riding on Bucephalus and would pause to compare notes and to lend encouragement. Sometimes three or four of the Nashes would come to sit for an hour under the juniper tree and to "chirk me up" with fun and kindliness—not to speak of the huge red apples that they shed on each occasion. Sometimes Ben Franklin would come through, warm and busy and full of enthusiasm about his own first fruits. He had a first grain crop that year. Or Isaac Newton would pause diffidently to read me a prose poem of no uncertain merit.

On May Day I gave my first party. In the plenitude of eggs at Broadview and the scarcity of other things I had evolved a number of creations among which the egg pancake took first honors. On May Day then, in acknowledgment of much sweet hospitality enjoyed, I offered unlimited egg pancakes to those hardy souls among my friends who would undertake to scale Friar Butte with me. About twenty achieved both the summit and the pancakes and, by whatever curious source of inspiration moved, the whole party adjourned to the schoolhouse and organized a Sunday school—a Sunday school, moreover, that was to be no bromidic affair, as perhaps may appear later.

I had been diligently studying dry farming, especially by means of the bulletins of the state and county experiment stations, and had carefully selected grain and garden seed in accordance with their advice. An experiment of this first summer was a little crop of Milo Maize, cultivated by hand. It did not ripen in the short season, but yielded a prodigious amount of fodder. As soon as the temperature at midnight began to threaten frost, I cut this precious fodder—about six hundred pounds—

with the carving knife, and tied it in bundles. This little first crop, which was carefully stored for the winter, looking toward that dear hope for the following summer—a cow—was later devoured by the Old Oregonian's rapacious steers, during my absence from the place.

The garden throve, but before the close of the summer that little cloud, that had been no larger than a man's hand when I came to Broadview, had begun to darken the heavens. I refer to the jack rabbits. In the early summer, while wild growth was still plentiful and succulent, they kept their distance, but as soon as this began to crisp, they turned in upon the garden. Each night they took their toll and the daily growth failed to keep pace with them. I tried to induce Bingo to accept responsibility for the policing of the garden, but he was an old dog and this was a new trick. He scattered the rabbits in a wild rout when I sicked him on, but he could not be taught to watch. At length, I hit upon the plan of carrying my blankets down at bedtime and sleeping in the grass at the edge of the garden. Here, in spite of many a ghostly attack upon them, I often awoke to find Bingo curled in slumber at my feet and bright-eyed jacks nibbling their fill almost at arm's length. In the end, all of the later garden fell to them. Even the roots and tubers, which I left to be harvested in the fall, they cheerfully dug and devoured, almost to the last potato.

XVII

AUNT POLLY—PIONEER

"Do you know Mrs. Fadden?"

"Aunt Polly? Well, sure!"

"She is my near neighbor."

My charioteer smote his thigh, and turned to look me squarely in the face. "Gee! but you're the lucky——" He was about to say dog, of course, but pulled up in confusion. I accepted the slip as tribute to the comradeship that had been established between us during our fifty-mile ride from the railroad.

And now she sat beneath my juniper tree—Aunt Polly, a little wiry, work-worn, gray woman, with very brown, deep-set eyes like my dog's. I was a one-year-old homesteader, and Aunt Polly and I had arrived at an understanding. I was not a talebearer, and Aunt Polly had relaxed to-me-ward the inexorable jaw with which the pioneers are wont to guard the secrets of their generation, and had become for me the historian of the cattle country. Her eyes looked far out over the sage and juniper-covered slopes to the blue mountains beyond the river, and she visioned again old days for my benefit. She had heard by 'phone that I had had a fall from a borrowed horse, and had trotted over with a bottle of liniment and a pie. I had landed like a cat, and ignored the liniment, but was an appropriate subject for the pie.

"The little pig died," said Aunt Polly mournfully, "that's why I didn't come sooner. The dogs hurt it yesterday an' it died this morning—a right nice little pig."

"Too bad," I said.

"Yes," responded Aunt Polly meditatively, "but them that has must lose."

Then she brightened, smoothing down her apron. "There's agoin' to be a candy pull on Nora Stimson, Sat'day. You must be ready an' we'll come by. Seems like she's been sort o' 'fended cause they've had s'prises on everybody else an' ain't never had none on her. So they're goin' to give her a candy-pullin'. Madden's baby swallowed a cartridge—a twenty-two. They had Doc Andrews, but he ain't got it."

I ventured the sally that the Madden baby might regard a cartridge as his natural nourishment. The Maddens are all sharp shots, and tradition has it that when game is scarce, the neighbors' stock is none too safe.

Aunt Polly regarded me with puzzled gravity, facetiousness being quite out of her line, but presently she accorded me a tardy "Mebbe." Then she smoothed the apron again. (This gesture recorded the paragraphs of the telephone bulletin.)

I steered Aunt Polly toward the relation of a history that she had frequently promised me—how she came to the country thirty years ago.

"It was April when we come," she said. "Yes, from The Dalles, two hundred miles. We'd heerd there'd be grass for the stock by then, so we'd waited. We was on the road eighteen days, 'count o' the stock. There was calves born on the way. We settled ten miles from neighbors, in the edge o' the pine timber. An' we hadn't more'n got the tent up 'fore Pauline (she called it Po-line) was born."

I gasped.

"Yes. I'd overstrained myself an' she come too soon. She never knowed the difference, though." Aunt Polly smiled as was her wont when "Po-line" was mentioned—gallant, gay-hearted Pauline, now the mother of her own little brood of advancing proportions.

"Next morning but one there was a foot o' snow, an' Fadden sure had a time!" I wondered about *Mrs.* Fadden in the ten-by-twelve tent, with four riotous boys and the new baby.

"We lost some stock. They wasn't used to it then." This apologetically, as for the weak fiber of stock in those early days. Well, I knew they were used to it now, having surreptitiously forked many a bunch of hay across the fence to the hungry-eyed Fadden calves.

"Soon as I was up, we set out sawing logs. All that summer we sawed logs an' boards—yes, whip-sawin' like—for the settlers that come. We was nearest to the timber. We made shakes, too. In between, we built our house, an' fenced fifteen acres for fodder an' garden. Yes, I dug many a post hole, an' set the post alone, but it's best for two to do it. One can hold while t'other tamps.

"Graters' folks come in that summer an' Pikes'—best o' friends they was—come together. You know what they are now."

"What was the matter, Aunt Polly?" Aunt Polly drew a long breath, reminded herself that I am not a tale-bearer, and proceeded.

"Graters' had a steer was always in Pikes' garden. Pike vowed he'd kill him. Run him clear to our dooryard one day an' shot him there. Pike hauled him off into the sagebrush. The coyotes ate him, an' Grater never knowed for a year what come of him."

"You didn't tell!"

Aunt Polly opened her eyes at me. "Sure not! Wouldn't nobody tell a thing like that."

"But it was a kind of crime, Aunt Polly."

Aunt Polly gave my objection not the slightest consideration. She answered shortly, "We don't," and continued. (In passing, for how many of our established customs can we give a better reason?

"We do" or "we don't," that is all. And it all dates back—but that is quite another story.)

"About a year after that, Grater was to our house one day an' my little Joe comes to me an' says, quite loud, 'It were Jim Grater's steer what Lon Pike killed by our gate, warn't it, Ma?' Grater give one look an' put out for home. That night there was six sheep killed in Lon Pike's corral. A week later Grater lost a horse, an' then Pike a cow. An' so they kep' it up—killin' more'n they raised some years.

"Then Brother Summy comes out an' holds tent meetin' an' a baptizin'. That's when *I* was baptized." (Aunt Polly smoothes her apron with a little smile, as of one who has closed one troublesome account.) "He worked on Pike an' Grater particular, he'd heerd about 'em; but it didn't seem to do no good till, down on the river bank, they comes up an' shakes hands, an' goes down into the water together. That held for quite a while, though you could see they was gettin' riled again. An' then come the dance."

"The dance?" Aunt Polly suggests a topic and waits to have it adopted before she dilates upon it.

"Harrisons built the first big house, an' give a dance for a house-warmin'. There was lots o' drinkin'. Sally Harrison herself can drink with the men. Her an' young Sally was both drunk, an' some o' the men was right wild. Well, when Pikes got home, Annie—she was a young girl not more'n sixteen—warn't with 'em. Too crazy to know it they was when they left. Next day, when she warn't to be found, it turned out Dick Grater was missin', too.

"Lon Pike swore it was human killin' this time, an' he got out with his gun.

"Then come Dick an' Annie in the night, beggin' us for a horse to go to town an' get married. There was a little old brandin' shack up in our timber. That's where they'd been, three days."

"You knew it!"

"Fadden seen them."

I remembered "We don't," and said nothing.

"They come back a week later with stificat' all fixed up with date same as night o' the dance. The old folks mistrusted, likely. They ain't spoke since, but everybody else s'poses it were straight."

So that was Mrs. Grater, with the rather high chin and patronizing air, and this little brown-eyed woman before me was the sole and sufficient guardian of her good name! In spirit I saluted humbly.

"One day in meetin'," continued Aunt Polly, "Annie Grater said something about a poor young orphan thing that was mistreated here among us, an' was for sendin' her out of the country. I just turned clear 'round an' give her one look, an' she dropped like a busted bubble."

"How long since the schoolhouse was built, Aunt Polly?"

"Fifteen years. Fadden an' me made the shakes an' cut a part of the logs. Everybody helped, an' when it was done, we had the first basket social!"

I suppressed a groan, but, glancing at Aunt Polly, I saw the event was one of true historic importance. It was as if one had mentioned the making of the first book, or the invention of the art of printing.

"Everybody just covered their boxes with white paper an' tied them with little bows." Aunt Polly smiled over the simplicity of those early days.

"I'd like to have been there," I said. My heart was still heavy with the memory of the *last* basket social with its funereal monuments of crêpe paper and paper flowers.

Aunt Polly missed my irony as I intended she should. "It *was* a right nice time," she said.

Upon one subject Aunt Polly is still reserved even with me—the character of the late Mr. Fadden, but, by implication, he was no saint.

"That's when the saloon come to Danes' Flat," she said once. "We was gettin' along before then."

"There ain't much about a man that I don't know," she remarked at another time, "an' I've no use for one whatever." She regards her four stalwart sons, who are devoted to her, with a cynical fondness that is unfathomable.

It is in the midst of this circle of sons that Aunt Polly is at her best. When I go to return the pie-plate, filled with shining, white, thoroughbred eggs, I hear Aunt Polly ranting, with the voice of a man, while I am yet afar off.

"Or I'll take it out of you!" These are her last words as I open the door.

"I'm givin' 'em the devil," she explains, turning an unbending countenance upon me. "Look at 'em. I want to kill 'em!"

The four stalwart sons sit about the table playing cards, and look up with broad and benevolent smiles. They adore Aunt Polly and they know there's many a stroke of work awaiting them, but what's the hurry?

Aunt Polly accepts the plate and gives me a cordial welcome, but ignores the eggs. The Pioneers give royally, but accept with a bad grace.

We all fall to the discussion of agriculture and of the promising condition of stock. I am told of the probable increase of the coming year and of the vicissitudes of the past. On the wall above the youths as they sit, hangs a glittering armory which represents the joy and pride of their being to a far greater extent than their tilled fields and browsing stock. And they love to kill, these tawny sons of Jacob, these herdsmen and shepherds and men of the chase, with an avidity that makes one tremble.

"Reckon Mis' Dunham won't get her house up

this fall. Ain't got men to haul her lumber." Mrs. Dunham is a widow and newcomer, and is living in a tent. My gaze touches upon the four muscular men and passes on out of the window to the herd of many horses grazing on the slopes, taking in, in the near foreground, wagons and harness for every purpose. Yet Mrs. Dunham must watch the oncoming of winter, and despair of getting her lumber hauled. Again I recall "We don't," also certain sad and memorable experiences of my own first year, and am silent. One must let the Pioneers be kind in their own way. If Mrs. Dunham should succumb to the rigors of winter, not one of her new neighbors but would hitch up and drive twenty miles to the funeral, be it in a very blizzard. ("We do.") Moreover, the cattle country has its own way of looking after widowhood. It eliminates the condition.

XVIII

"TO-MORROW AND TO-MORROW AND TO-MORROW"

As the second autumn approached, my arrangements for seeding the new ground having been made, and a teaching position offering in Prineville, I decided to close Broadview for the winter and move into town. I procured a tent house and chicken yard on the edge of town and lived there throughout the teaching term, finding an excellent market for eggs and chickens. Each week-end I rode out to Broadview to sleep—a sixty-mile round trip, in which I delighted as often as a really good horse was available. About the fifteenth of October I found my grain all in. I am glad to chronicle that this feat was at last accomplished by one of the pioneers—a son of Aunt Polly. About the first of November I found my chicken house in ruins and my milo maize evaporated—seemingly by the ever-thirsty atmosphere, since not a scrap or shadow of a leaf remained. On one Saturday night an early blizzard caught me on the homestead. All night I lay and shivered in my rocking tent house and all night my poor horse stamped and whinnied under a tree near by. With morning came the sunshine and a glorious day for my return to town. On another occasion I faced one of those fierce periodic winds, which, while usually warm, it is well-nigh impossible to stand against. I crouched low upon my horse and clung to the saddle, while my good steed plodded slowly with bent head, and dust, in towering columns, met, enveloped, and passed us by. I learned that day how long is thirty miles at a foot pace. With the coming of real winter, I claimed my five months' leave of absence and saw Broadview no more until early spring. On that occasion I took a party of gay young teachers for a night's camp and greatly enjoyed their envious appreciation of my luxuriant first crop and of Broadview landscapes very lovely in the spring sunshine.

On Easter morning, I being at Broadview for the week end, Mary Porter gave a little breakfast for me. Isaac Newton came over from the Basin. Ben Franklin rode over. The morning was very mild and lovely and we breakfasted before the open door from which we could look far down the Crooked River over the softening, uncertain-tinted landscape of spring. One at least of the breakfasters felt no hunger for church and cowl the better to celebrate the resurrection of Nature. Several of the party escorted me some miles on my way and I recall that we found the Easter rabbits—a wee brood of little jacks peeping out from under a clump of sage. Reason said destroy them in their early infancy, but it was a day of life, not death, and they got no harm from us.

With the close of school, I returned in earnest to the life of a farmer. Again the incubator ran constantly. Again the garden—increased now to two acres to accommodate experiments with field peas and dry-land alfalfa. These two acres I worked by hand, obtaining excellent results except for that ever-increasing menace—the multiplying jack rabbit. I was a proud farmer when the first shiny automobile drew up to my door and the county agriculturist spent an hour going over my place with me, advising and commending, leaving when he departed a goodly store of seeds for further experimentation. The field peas particularly yielded an elegant crop, the solid low hedges of the vines meeting at last across the rows and intertwining, forming cool, dark arcades through which my multitudinous little chicks chirped and twittered, catching great numbers of insects, themselves in rare safety from the preying hawks.

It was a good summer and my first wheat crop came to maturity without mishap. This was no common experience—this first fruition of oft-blighted hopes. It inspired a mild rhapsody in my Journal:

"The possession of ancestral acres is bound up with sentiment, yet an inheritance of virgin soil bestows an inspiration of its own. How the centuries have toiled, through fire and frost and wind and wave and springing life and long decay to lay these fields so wide and deep! None but the last word of agricultural science is worthy to govern their disturbance. They alone among the fields of earth have suffered neither neglect nor ignorance nor folly, neither over-fattening nor depletion. Reverent as Adam we should come to them and with far greater skill. 'Tis wonderful—a first crop—a greening field of one's own producing. One feels a new sympathy with the Creator. And, as it reaches up—the growing grain—how one loves to walk through it, to hear it rustle about one's knees, and to watch the wind waves ripple over it. Golden, ready for the harvest, it is beyond words, and in the stack it is the most tangible of the fruits of industry—bread of life for man and beast and for many a winged sojourner and bright-eyed burrower in the soil!"

A Puritan childhood, a youth nourished largely upon Emerson and the poets, and a purely professional career possibly do not forewarn or forearm one quite adequately for practical business experience. A tendency to an idealistic view of human motives and human conduct was strengthened in the Pilgrim by all of that generous largeness and openness of Nature in her western phase—that high, clear, sparkling countenance, daily familiarity with which would seem to compel frankness, openness, and generosity in the human soul. Beneath the juniper tree, it seemed inevitable to take one's neighbors at their own valuation—to believe that what seemed guilelessness, simplicity, and disinterested benevolence was actually such. Time and the happy harvesting of my first crop had dulled the edge of earlier disappointments and disillusionments, when the serpent once more raised his wily head.

A new law for semi-arid regions had doubled the allowance of land to the homesteader and I had taken another desirable one hundred and sixty adjoining the first. This necessitated the breaking of the second twenty acres. A young man—a new settler—riding in company with his young wife, paused at the tent house door and applied for the job. He was of childlike though muscular appearance and of docile mien. Immediately I warmed to the young pair. I had a fellow-feeling for all beginning-homesteaders. I presented the plowman with free pasture for his term of work—fenced pasture being of no negligible value in this overstocked, short-grass country. I went with the contractor to the scene of action. I outlined the projected field. I dwelt upon all essential details of the work desired. Then, in accordance with my idea of proper confidence in the employed, I left the matter in his hands.

Months proved insufficient to reveal the full extent of Mephistophelian intelligence that underlay this youth's bland and infantile expression. Arithmetic that would have fifteen acres equal twenty; geometry that would have a circle appear a square; mechanics that produced the effect of plowing without the reality; sagebrush clearing that left a clean surface while all the brush was retained in the conspiring soil; so-called uprooted junipers skilfully struck from their clinging bases two inches beneath the surface of the soil. The harrow, the seeder, again the harrow upon the tender crop, the mower, the rake and the hay wagon—each contributed to exhibit the perfidy of the wily innocent, and left portions of themselves upon the field as witnesses to their Herculean struggles with the mountainous and snag-infested soil.

Through the multiplication of examples, I became protestingly familiar with the methods of my first contractor. Perhaps it was a ripe crop needing the harvester, winter staring one in the face and no woodpile, hungry stock and a depleted stack yard. All inquiries would seem to fall upon deaf ears till —late in time—some gentle hypocrite would become solicitous. Magnifying the difficulties in his way, he would consent, from pure neighborliness, to lend a helping hand in my dilemma. And when the bill came in—a top-notch price—so great had been my need that I paid it with unquestioning gratitude.

Seed wheat was to be brought from town; the ground waited and frost threatened. A reluctant neighbor volunteered for the arduous task. He consumed four days in the sixty-mile round trip—representing that mercy to his team demanded that amount of time. Five dollars per day for man and team was the compensation asked. (These were ante-bellum prices.) It was the full price of the wheat. When I learned in a later and slightly wiser period of existence, that two of the four days had been squandered upon a spree in town, I set down among my mental notes: "Experience—ten dollars."

An item in the Journal during this summer records an event of some moment in our little circle:

"Mary Porter slipped off the other day and married Andrew DeLong. They went for a little wedding journey to see her people near Chicago. Andrew has never been out of the county before, but I know the haughty eye that he turned upon each new experience. Ben Franklin had the new homesteaders to dine to-day in Mary's honor. Ben Franklin's little house is a model of neatness and convenience, and to see him make biscuit—"sour dough" of course—and fruit pudding, and cook his lavish dinner to a turn while calmly acting the host and entertainer, was a reproach to some one I know, all indifferent to her housekeeping duties. Mary is in the seventh heaven, of course, and we all had to be patient with her idealizing of Andrew, whom we have regarded as just a common man. Both are elevated for the moment at least by each other's adoration, and have a shiny look about them that sobers us independents.

"Isaac Newton walked home with me in the late afternoon and I had some good talk with him such as I have with no one else. He is always absorbed in one philosophic problem or another. His favorite speculations have to do with telepathy. He had the indiscretion to propound some of these on one occasion in conversation with the 'Old Oregonian' and has gained thereby the reputation of being 'off his nut,' as I heard it expressed. No doubt at all but his transcendental ancestry is at work in him. The reputation referred to is not at all helped by his absent-mindedness. He started for Ben Franklin's one evening, got to thinking and lost himself. It was pitchy black when he began to look for landmarks, and, finding none, slept under a juniper or, rather, *waked* there until dawn. 'My, but I had some good thought that night,' he says. One thing that he never forgets is to do the opportune and thoughtful deed for his friends, as I can warmly testify."

As early as August I had arranged with a neighbor who was yet to be tested to harrow my new ground and to put in a forty-acre crop at a safe date in the fall. By mid-October I was growing anxious and called around from time to time to see him and to urge the danger of an early freeze. He had taken on one job after another and had been prevailed upon to see these through and to leave mine till the last. My explanation of much of my difficulty along this line is that the labor of men in the country is reciprocal—each man in helping another is establishing a definite bank account for himself in time of need, and, on the same principle, failure to accommodate means retaliation when it may be most sorely felt. Frost came and came to stay. The ground was soon as hard as rock and once more my seed wheat lay through the winter—a sad reminder of fruitless planning.

I had decided to stay by the place this second winter. I had, for the first time, my own wheat for the chickens and I had hoped that they would yield me sufficient income for my small needs. It was a rash decision. Mid-winter found me not only penniless but in debt. The unplanted seed was to be paid for and the dallying neighbor pressed for payment for the partial work he had put in. This cropping experience taught me the worthlessness of a written contract without penalty. It was in black and white that my forty-acre seeding should be complete and ready for winter by October fifteenth. The party of the first part having failed absolutely in his agreement, I had no redress, no compensation whatever for my cropless year, while he could collect wages for every day of labor that he had put in.

Being penniless, I had no wood put in, but continued to depend upon my own daily exertions, although available fuel was retreating always further from the fire, for even one lone homesteader can burn a huge amount of wood in the course of two years' time. I cut dry purshia and juniper just where I found it and carried it in sacks to the tent house. This went very well until, one midwinter morning, a foot of snow and zero temperature suggested the realities of life. For a solid month, while the mercury hovered about zero—for it was an exceptional winter—I dug my wood out of the steadily accumulating snow and carried it home upon my back for the scant comfort and respite of an hour's fire. On one dreadful day, I burned my chopping block, which was a relic of a present of a wagon load of pine that Ben Franklin and Andrew DeLong had brought me in the fall and that I had gaily and lavishly burned. On the next day—the blizzard continuing—I burned my ladder, and on the next would have sacrificed my steps, had not a blessed chinook blown up in the night, carried the snow away in foaming torrents, and laid bare many a rich and unsuspected treasure of fuel.

My good friends knew little of my difficulties during this memorable month. The snow had isolated us all in our rough back-country. The only family that passed and saw anything of my mining for fuel in the frozen drifts were connected with one of my faithless contractors and were bearing themselves haughtily on the principle that one bad turn deserves another. I knew what it was during this winter to lack two cents for postage. My letters had to await the pleasure of the hens, who had troubles of their own during the severe weather and almost ceased to lay. Toward spring a loan—that wolf in sheep's clothing, whose day of reckoning is sure—gave immediate relief and spring opened once more glad and hopefully.

Possibly, however, the hardships of the winter had temporarily weakened the fiber, for I find a pensive note in the Journal on the subject of love in Nature. I take it that this was before I had got to work with the hoe and before the first brood of biddies had peeped:

"The ice is gone out of the river with a great uproar and a bridge or two. Spring is suddenly upon us wholeheartedly and permanently, it would seem. Everywhere grass is greening, and purshia shrubs are alive with bees and heavy with perfume. The land is noisy with the bleating and lowing of herds being separated for summer pasture. Some are already on the mountains and the high challenge of their leaders comes to me now and again. Bluebirds complain and hover about my little house till I put up a dwelling for them, with sad misgivings as to Kitty Kat. Robins and flickers search out their nesting sites as near to human habitation as may be, daring cats in preference to hawks. Everywhere is vocal stir and movement, restlessness and change. And the heart of an old maid is restless, too, and her thoughts are long, long thoughts. For a few weeks the turbulence and excitement, the seeking and the loving—the high tide of individual existence—then the long, long peace and brooding and devotion—looking toward the natural end of this universal impulse—the repopulating of the earth.

"And we, who call ourselves the lords of all, who alone among the tribes of earth may not freely follow the urge of spring, have we found a more excellent way? Does the lawful home fully justify the position of the voluntary celibates or the position of that vast body of brothers and sisters who do follow the urge of spring, but by stealth and with deception and with all the accompaniment of ignominy, disgrace, and degradation that the law-abiding can heap upon them? Must they who fear the lifelong bond—those to whom the thought that spontaneity might become obligation is intolerable—be forever denied this spark of life, this high experience of love and union, in order that the benediction of the 'blessed condition' may rest upon the prosaic multitude, uninspired and uninspiring?

"A few times in a lifetime comes a great friend to light our spirit with fresh flame from the altar—to be incorporated into the substance of our lives. Why not the same with love? And the fruit of spontaneous love—the little child? A precious jewel, to be of all things treasured."

This was to be my most eventful summer. On my birthday in June came a check for fifty dollars from a good relative who had become interested in my curious way of life. It happened that just at this time a valuable Jersey cow whose record I well knew was offered at the unusual price of sixty-five dollars. Her owners were leaving the country and must dispose of her.

My check spent only one night at Broadview, and, two or three days later, "Bossy" was driven within the confines of her new home, and stood knee deep in the June grass, eying me with habitual suspicion and defiance.

I venture here, since Bossy became at once and continued to be so large a personage at Broadview, to include, intact, a brief biography that I was moved to write, some seasons later. If this disturbs too much the continuity of my simple tale, may I be forgiven.

XIX

BOSSY AND PSALMMY

WHEN Bossy came to Broadview she was very near to maternity—a happy circumstance, I had thought—yet I was appalled at the tragic hopelessness of her eyes and the aloof distrustfulness of all her ways. Casting about for an explanation, I hit, I believe, upon the true one. Bossy had been a town cow kept for milk alone, which means that the joy of motherhood had been for her of but a few hours' duration, followed by a sleepless day and night of crying out for that of which she had been bereft, and then dull acceptance of the fate decreed.

Free roaming in a big pasture was a new experience, and she quite evidently delighted in the most remote corners, the shade of the spreading junipers, and the hidden hollows among the boulders. It was a time when I felt I must keep a watchful eye upon her to see that all went well, so daily, in Bingo's wake, I sought her out, notwithstanding that our solicitude was received by her with every demonstration of wrath and displeasure. Springing to her feet at our approach she would lower her head ominously and proceed to paw the earth and to envelop herself in a fine cloud of volcanic ash as if, like certain of the immortals, she were about to depart invisibly.

But the morning came at last when my eyes descried from afar a wee, wabbly, tan-colored mite at her side, upon which her head rested, while her watchful eyes were already upon us with an unwinking attention. Somewhat to my surprise she accepted from the first, though without cordiality, my right to touch and handle the calf, but with a sudden fierce rush she bowled over poor old Bingo, thereby hurting his feelings irretrievably. He had been always restrained and entirely considerate in his attitude toward her. The calf, to my great regret, was a little steer, yet with such promise of beauty and delightfulness that I promptly forgot his one disqualification.

For four days Bossy was left in undisturbed possession, except that each day I drove her to the home enclosure and insisted upon making the calf's acquaintance for the purposes of the future. On the fifth day, I had decided, the separation such as it was to be must come, but, while I must do the practical thing from the standpoint of an embryo dairyman, Bossy should still have the privilege of access to that which she held so dear and the satisfaction of knowing of his welfare and contentment. ("It is a hymn," I had written my mother on the day of his birth. "Call him Psalmmy then, southern pronunciation," she wrote back. So "Psalmmy" or Sammy he became.) On the fifth day then, Bossy being for precaution's sake both tied and corralled, I slipped a little halter on Psalmmy and gave him his first lesson in leading, he struggling and choking madly the while and "blatting" piteously, yet following with wabbly impotence in my wake till safely secured in his little straw-bedded pen beside Bossy's stall in the shed.

And Bossy? She bellowed and pawed; she flung up her tail; she fell upon her knees and gouged the earth with the roots of her vanished horns; she flung ashes upon her head and, metaphorically, rent her garments from neck to hem. Trembling, I approached and released her, having left the corral gate conveniently open for her exit. Like a stampeded buffalo, with nose to ground, she dashed on the trail of the vanished calf, entering the shed a whirlwind of wrath and tragedy. But there was little Psalmmy all unhurt, trotting about his pen and reaching his little wet nose to her, his whole silky little self quite within reach of her comforting tongue.

Thus a most contented season was inaugurated. The regular milkings satisfied Bossy's most urgent physical need, and Psalmmy's immediate presence, where he might still be licked and loved, satisfied her mother heart. There was plenty of milk and cream for Psalmmy and for me. Bossy's eyes grew soft and gentle, her attitude trustful. Autumn rains kept the grass growing and Bossy allowed herself to wander farther and farther from the shed till at last she would remain out all day, though subject to fits of panic when she heard the bark of a strange dog or unknown voices about the barn. Then she would come crashing through the sagebrush with a low and ominous bellowing and all the old apprehension in her eyes. Even after a quiet day of grazing, when she came over the last ridge and within sight of the barn, she would break into a run and, with murmurings solicitous and low, seek the goal of her desire—little Psalmmy, chewing contentedly on his alfalfa, eager but not suffering for her caresses.

And as for Psalmmy and me? I had never raised a little calf. From the time that I first felt the urgent curl of his little tongue about my fingers in the pail of warm milk till, in the days of his maturity, he would still lay his head upon my shoulder, stretching his great neck that I might caress its velvet folds, the experience was a delight. Beautiful to ideality with his great fawn's eyes, his coat soft as a seal's, his exquisite harmonies of tans and browns, and his winning, confidently affectionate nature, he stood, moreover, for health and peace and quietness and substantiality. He was one of those animals with whom Whitman desired to turn and live.

For the first weeks of his early infancy Bossy never failed to turn from her newly-filled manger to watch the process of milk-drinking, intent but satisfied, and gradually she developed an affection for me because I cared for Psalmmy. When Bossy was gone to pasture, Psalmmy followed me about the place, constantly bumping into me in his eagerness to keep close, and planting his sharp little hoofs in the tops of my low shoes with excruciating effect. When I went indoors, he would bump against the door as I disappeared and would remain for some moments sucking the door-knob, his great eyes rolled upward to the little window in the door at which I paused to look down upon him. Very early in his life he developed a note of greeting with which he never failed to acknowledge my return after any excursion. Discovering my approach, he would run to the nearest point that intervening fences permitted, then would brace his feet, hump his little back, draw in his chin, bow his neck, and, with a seemingly tremendous effort, would bring forth a guttural "b-a-a-a-w!" that moved me both to tears and laughter.

One day in the late winter Psalmmy slipped a bar in his pen and I returned from an excursion to find him sporting somewhat drunkenly in the wake of his mother as she sauntered about the place. It was then that I discovered that Psalmmy was not weaned, as I had fondly trusted. His lips were foamy with the amplitude of the beverage in which he had indulged and, quite evidently, Bossy had reserved nothing for my personal needs. Upon another and another occasion the same condition was demonstrated and it became evident that, with the coming of spring and pasture, some method of forcible prohibition must be inaugurated. I decided upon a basket muzzle and presently turned the two out together on the tender grass. For several days all went well. Psalmmy came dutifully to his feeding pail for his just portion, and Bossy filled my flowing bowl with yellowing richness.

One evening I was delayed at the milking hour. Psalmmy became ravenous, Bossy impatient. Through experimentation it was discovered that if Psalmmy turned his head upside down the muzzle would fall backward, leaving his mouth unhampered. This, of course, was the end of the efficacy of the basket muzzle. I then, not without keen regret and self-reproach, procured a spiked one. Once more, for a day or two, the milk was saved. Then I came upon the two in the pasture, Bossy chewing the cud of supreme content, Psalmmy, having learned to lay the spikes so skillfully and with such infinite deliberation against Bossy's tender flesh as to cause her no inconvenience, imbibing with closed eyes and deep-drawn sighs of satisfaction. I amplified the defensive armor with fiendish barbed wire entanglements and mighty nails. I devised hitherto unpatented muzzles and barricades. I tried to envelop Bossy in a protective covering. I applied a paste of salve and a saturated solution of red pepper. My efforts were as chaff before the wind of their inflamed desire. They endured all hardness. Psalmmy smacked his lips over the fiery sauce that was the condition of his repast.

Nothing remained but to put a fence between them. This I did, once more with compassion and remorse. For a day or two they lowed mournfully to one another through the bars. Then they conspired again. Regularly at luncheon time Bossy drew near to the fence, and Psalmmy, with his nose thrust through a convenient gap, drank long and deep. I tried another fence. I tried another pasture. I tried the government reserve twenty miles distant. Always sundown of a day sooner or later arrived at brought Bossy and Psalmmy peacefully home together, Bossy released of her rich and ample load, Psalmmy rolling in his gait and stupid to inebriety. No wires were too closely set, no gate too high, no location too distant for the ingenuity or the valor of his ruling passion.

"Beef him!" counseled my neighbors brutally. "It's all he's good for, anyway. What are you keeping him for?" What *was* I keeping him for? Theory and practice were all against me. Yet, when Psalmmy humped his back and uttered his joyous "b-a-a-a-w" at my approach, or laid his silken cheek to mine and I felt the warm folds of his neck, I was weak as water in the hands of fate. Anyway, he was not yet two years old. Even practical stock men kept calves that length of time, and, besides, I was counting upon the coming of another calf for the effectual weaning of Psalmmy.

Vain hope. For a brief season Psalmmy did not suck. Then, when the new calf had been relegated to Psalmmy's little pen, Bossy took Psalmmy once more to her heart and they strolled the fields together. It was a sight to make the most melancholy hold their sides with laughter—Bossy chewing the cud, her dreamy eyes seeing, as it were, "some far-off divine event," and Psalmmy—great, lusty fellow that he was, quite outclassing her in size—stooping for his native draught with all the ardor and, at the same time, meek dependence of a calfling. In the end, I built a Psalmmy-proof fence, raising it higher and higher till he was at last outdone.

XX

FLY

ONLY a few weeks after the advent of Bossy another equally momentous addition was made to my family circle. Entries in the Journal poorly suggest the enthusiasm engendered thereby:

"This has been a day of days. I've bought a horse! I can't realize it yet, can't believe it! I have to go to the window every few minutes to see her grazing there—my beautiful white mare! I have to open my door and gloat over my russet saddle and bridle hanging on the porch. By virtue of my school salary I have been able to bank my egg money for some time past, looking toward some special investment. There are a dozen needs for which it seemed equally appropriate. At last count I had an even fifty dollars. I hadn't let myself entertain for a moment the thought of achieving a horse as yet.

"This morning my neighbor, Myles Nash, rode in while I was feeding the chicks. I have always greatly admired his mare, 'Fly,' and have had several memorable rides on her. She is a broncho, but exceptionally well-broken and of a very friendly and affectionate nature. She has beautiful, great eyes as expressive as a human's.

"Myles dismounted and handed me the bridle. 'I want to sell you my horse,' he said.

" 'What's the matter with her?' I asked.

"He looked teased at that and I was sorry. He is one of the salt of the earth, and my good friend. 'The matter's with me,' he said. 'I'm called away. Important changes and matters for me to settle. There's just no telling when, if ever, I shall come back. I want you to take Fly for her sake and yours too, if you'll let me say so, and I need the money. Even fifty for horse, saddle, bridle, and blanket just as they stand.' I gasped. One couldn't touch either of the first two for twice that sum.

" 'Done!' I said as soon as I got my breath. I went into the house and made out a check. Myles unsaddled Fly and turned her out, then drove a huge nail under the shelter of the porch and hung up the trappings. He's more tender of the latter than ever I shall be. After he had gone I sat down on the steps, literally weak from excitement. I was hot all over and my heart was beating inconveniently.

"Fly has ushered in a new heaven and a new earth. She has given wings to my spirit and motive power to my most serious activities. For three years I have been carrying a good part of my supplies on my back—often thirty to forty pounds—for three and a half miles. Of course an occasional passing wagon has helped me out. For the same length of time I have cut and carried in sacks most of my wood, with the exception of a slight investment in the winter. All of my neighborhood errands have, of necessity, been done on foot. I have become a sort of grayhound, often covering ten to fifteen miles in the day's incidentals.

"But now my weary journeyings have become a flight—a joy and stimulus—a mere expression of my delight in the homestead life. And, with a beast of burden, I unload my firewood at the door—three or four times my accustomed load and I as fresh as a daisy. I intend to plan for some light cultivating machinery that will save much of the back-breaking work in my two-acre garden, also for a light wagon for my hauling."

XXI

THE COMPANIONS

WHEN tradition gave way to science, and evolution took the place of special creation, the human race came into a new heritage. Man found himself, in no figurative sense, "heir of the ages." His sympathies began to expand, and became commensurate with the universe. A vast brotherhood with other species became evident, and, very slowly, his world-old arrogance became modified. If he possessed qualities that had made him dominant over all other races, still not in all qualities did he excel. Very slowly he has come to see that certain admirable traits may be better represented by the dog under the table than by his gluttonous master. Not only must we consider the superiority of the dog's senses and of his muscular response, but no human can rival his sympathetic intuition or the depth and faithfulness of his affections.

To those who have consciously come into this new heritage the companionship of animals is enhanced in value. We value love as love, sympathy as sympathy, and the thousand responses of our furred and feathered friends become of interest and value.

The Companions

When Whitman declared his half-formed intention to "turn and live with the animals" he was in poetic mood, yet very literally can it be done with profit and rest to the soul. Poor Nebuchadnezzar—his skull dented with the weight of the crown, and his spirit harassed by the irksomeness and folly of his state—found in a seven-year exile with the beasts of the field, and in the blessings of the dew of heaven, the cure of his soul.

People say to me that it must be desolate, living alone at Broadview. I reply that I am not alone. I am conscious of no lack—at least in the region of our simpler and more fundamental thoughts and feelings—of reciprocal understanding and sympathy. To and fro at my side on all of my busy excursions about the farm, trot Bingo and Kitty Kat—interested observers of all my activities, happy in their own digressive explorations and fruitful hunts, ever ready in my moments of rest with eloquent companionship and tender caress, drawing close with me at the close of day by the fireside or on the doorstone, sharing the peace of evening after the busy day. My chickens gather in little groups about me as I work here and there, engaging me in cheery conversation, essaying little familiarities and friendly overtures, even performing certain stunts with self-conscious gravity, delighting in personal attention. Fly—joy of my life, swift, tireless companion of my larger adventures—accommodates her browsing to my movements, keeping me in sight with that undemonstrative friendliness characteristic of her kind. Bossy—silky-coated Jersey, producer of foamy milk and golden butter—with all her impatient head-tossings and waywardness under control, still feeds the home end of the pasture quite into the ground, rather than follow better grazing out of sight of our domestic circle.

There is that in the gentle response of these calm and friendly creatures that soothes the spirit and leaves the mind free for its own excursions. Not so with the harassing companionship of non-understanding humans. The cheerful care-freedom of the animals is contagious. It harmonizes with all out-of-doors, and engages one's own spirit in the unapprehensive activities of Nature. All Nature is cheerful till calamity befalls, and the calamities of Nature are short and sharp, and cloud the heavens of the immediate victims only.

XXII

THE SURVIVAL OF THE FITTEST

A SAWMILL had been set up in the Maury Mountains only six miles distant. It was employing a good-sized force and gave me a home market for eggs. Now that I had stock I needed a barn, and my own little domicile was going to pieces. During this summer I traded enough eggs for lumber for house and barn, and two of the immortals in my grateful memory—Andrew DeLong and Ben Franklin—suspended their own operations long enough to erect them for me. These neighborhood offices were, of course, on a business basis, but in the early years on a homestead a man's time never goes begging and I had learned to be warmly grateful for all such service.

My little house was of one room, twenty by twelve, facing east, the front, which was the long way of the room, having a broad porch. Upon this porch, in the center, opened a double door, and on each side of the door was a window two by four, the long way being horizontal and the window letting down against the wall on hinges. Thus, on summer days, it was possible to open the whole front of the house on to the shady porch. Below, set in this shadowy frame, extended the bright valley and beyond this my amethyst mountains glowed in ever-changing hues. Each end of the room had a square, hinged window high in the wall. One end of the long room I arranged with shelves and kitchen conveniences. The other held my cot, table, and book shelves. One passed imperceptibly from kitchen to parlor and there were no darkening and cramping partitions. Often, on a moonlight night, I thought the proportions of my room like a section of a parlor car. I fancied I could think better in my bright and airy quarters. They seemed to bestow a new fund of hope and imagination. The little barn was just large enough for roomy quarters for cow and calf and for two horses. Hay in this climate needs no shelter, and my stack was close at hand. I was thus at rest in the certainty that Fly and Bossy would be sheltered from the "cauld, cauld blast" and it was not very long, as the Journal records, before shelter was needed.

"I have been very watchful of my Fly of late, insisting that she sleep under cover, and providing her with a thick, clean, straw bed. This morning, when I went out to feed, there stood a brand-new black horse, exceedingly diminutive, at the manger, actually nibbling hay like an old stager. Fly was in a tumult of emotion. Her eyes blazed when I approached, and, when Bingo barked at a sage rat across the yard, she fell into violent trembling. She tried to keep her nose in contact with the funny, wabbly mite that is her daughter, and a time she had of it, for it is already as lively as a cricket. The colt showed fear of me and it took courage to go into the stall and handle it, with Fly's fiery eyes upon me. I knew I must establish my right to do so, and, like Bossy, Fly did not question it. I think it is their consciousness of dependence that leads them to commend their young to us, however great their anxiety may be."

A later item records the progress of my acquaintance with the latest comer:

"I have never dreamed of the sweetness of a little colt, have never thought it particularly attractive among baby creatures. But my little 'Babe'—Velvet Babe, I want to call her, for no seal was ever softer—is simply irresistible. She pricks up her ears and runs to me at sight, sounding her shrill little whinny—the same as when she sees her mother approaching. She lays her little silky cheek against mine when I stoop to pet her and leaves it there in the tenderest caress. She will be a beautiful saddler, they tell me, and I shall have the joy of raising her for myself. Her blackness is fast disappearing. She is now a light maltese, and they say she will be white. Every white horse begins life as a black one, I am assured. I have no way of verifying this."

Two other Journal notes of this year deal with some very real problems that the homesteader was up against—the jack rabbit and the mad coyote—and the thoughts on the world in general that they inspired.

"The 'problem of evil' in the theological sense has never concerned me greatly, nor have I ever had a proper 'sense of sin'—as certain dear Presbyterian friends have endeavored to make clear to me. I have always been conscious of an urge toward goodness and harmony rather than toward unrighteousness, and sin has seemed to me to be rather the result of a conflict of perfectly justifiable aims and tendencies than of total depravity at the source. Yet the problem of evil in another sense has given me many a bad hour. That feature of the world's organization according to which otherwise lovable and gracious creatures must 'eat each other up,' with all due accompaniments of agony, terror, and ferocity, cuts me to the very quick. And especially the necessity laid upon us lords of creation to 'rise, slay, and eat' or, at the very least, to rise and slay or be ourselves devoured remains for me unreconcilable with our capacity for pity and tenderness and with our ability to put ourselves in the other fellow's place even in the case of other species than our own.

"For years I was vegetarian, rather in obedience to feeling than principle, and I eat meat always under protest against the quality of mercy lodged within me. In fact the cruelties of life have darkened the world for me since my earliest recollection. My preoccupation with the fate of the sweet turtle doves, the little first lambs of the flock, the gentle heifers whose calves were tied at home while they 'ascended (lowing) to the hill of the Lord,' bearing the ark of the covenant, there to spill their own blood to placate Jehovah for the sins of men,—this preoccupation it was perhaps that prevented me (as a child) from learning to love the Lord my God, as in that connection depicted, with all my heart and mind and soul and strength. However, to come down to this year of our Lord nineteen-blank and to the ranchers' situation in Crook County Oregon:

"As I sit before my window on this late autumn afternoon and look down across sage-covered slopes toward the river valley, little dark objects appear and disappear, scurrying in every direction, and I know that Brer Jack Rabbit is only waiting for the fall of twilight in order that he and all his kin may assemble about our wheat and alfalfa stacks and thresh and feed with an appetite truly phenomenal.

For a thousand years, presumably, this vast plateau which is now my home has been covered with sagebrush and bunch grass and sprinkled with juniper trees, and has supported a normal population of jack rabbits and sage rats. Then suddenly comes man with his alien stock, his dogs and his cats, his new and succulent crops, with their admixture of weed seeds and germs of insect life. And, lo, this quiet and harmonious state of nature is all in turmoil.

"Sage and bunch grass give place to wheat and oats and varied vegetables. Strange creatures wander upon the ancient hills. The coyote tribe samples young lamb and thereupon begins to wax and grow fat and incidentally to prepare the way for its own extermination. Hawks become delirious over the chicken yards and neglect the young rabbits and sage rats. Rabbits and sage rats, largely relieved from the depredations of their ancient enemies, and suddenly supplied with new and luscious herbage in unlimited quantity, flourish and multiply beyond all reason. Short-sighted man spends the early years of his residence in feeding these inoffensive little denizens of the brush and in exterminating their enemies as rapidly as possible. Brer Rabbit and Sis Sage rat sample the grains and cast their vote in favor of wheat. They taste all products of the garden and, though finding them universally edible, cultivate a taste for lettuce and young peas and beans and sweet corn. Then, one morning, man awakes and finds that he can no longer raise wheat and garden products except with the greatest vigilance. The growth of each day is consumed nightly. Even his root crops, untouched through the early summer, are dug and devoured as autumn comes on. With the coming of winter the rabbits are with him still. They surround his stacks and thresh out enough grain each night to feed several head of stock.

"Rabbits have become what is termed 'a fearful pest' to the farmer. In my own case they ate one sixth of my crop last year, this year one third. They also did away with all fruitfulness in my garden, although I literally slept as well as waked with it. I held converse with myself and decided that I was showing myself unfit in the struggle for existence. I bought a "twenty-two" and set about defending my rights.

"The rabbits were very tame. That was the worst of it; they did not fear me. I had no trouble in knocking a few over. They looked surprised, were still a moment, then rolled over in convulsions and were still forever. It was a new and gruesome experience—being responsible for that. But in one case I broke a leg. This little victim also looked surprised and puzzled. He hopped a few paces, stopped and examined himself, and then hopped away into the brush, the ruined limb flopping and dangling behind him. I tried, but was unable to find him, to save him from the cruel fate I had visited upon him. In another instance, I broke a back. The victim tried to drag himself off the field, pawing desperately, his hind quarters entirely paralyzed. When I approached to end his sufferings with a charge of shot, he regarded me with bulging eyeballs and the trembling of hopeless terror. And I? I was filled with horror and amazement at the thing that I had done. I shall remember those two rabbits as long as life is mine. Still I use poison, a remedy that is swift and deadly, and merciful chiefly to myself.

"The method of destruction most in vogue is to draw a woven wire fence around the alfalfa stacks, arranging narrow chutes, easy of entrance but difficult of exit. When snow is on the ground, rabbits crowd into these little corrals in unbelievable numbers. In the morning, the rancher and his hired hands, with clubs and dogs, enter the enclosure for a bit of rare sport, laying about them right and left, afterward scalping the prostrate creatures for the bounty, recking not whether they be dead or alive. One of my neighbors thus killed three thousand in one snowy season. While I? I buy the poor mangled bodies at one cent each—four or five pounds of solid meat—and cook them for my biddies, making a wonderful bran and rabbit stew, magical in its effect upon egg production. A young jack rabbit is very good eating, but, largely I imagine, because of the abundance of beef and mutton, partly too as a consequence of a peculiar disease found among the mature rabbits, rabbit flesh is very unpopular in the ranch country. A rabbit eater would expose himself to a goodly measure of contempt.

"The 'rabbit drive' is older than the corral method and is a favorite pastime. The neighborhood unites—usually on a Sunday—decides upon some favorable place—usually a gully—as the end of the drive, and incloses this in an angle of woven wire with sides extending out a good distance in the form of a chute. Then the country is beaten up by a wide half circle of beaters, the rabbits being driven toward and into the chute. The enclosure of wire is then made complete and the clubbing and dogging follow, as in the case of the hay stack procedure. A big dinner at some near-by rancher's constitutes 'the end of a perfect day.' A rabbit cries very pitifully and humanly when hurt and not killed. It is said that it was difficult at first to get men to do the clubbing because of this feature and the exceeding gentleness of the animal. All such qualms are now, however, a thing of the past. The privilege is much sought after."

The Journal account of the mad coyote follows:

"One day last autumn, a man walking through

the timber to Maury's mill, only ten miles from here, was attacked from behind by a coyote, which sprang upon him and fastened its teeth in his hand. Running on before him in a dazed sort of way, the animal preceded him to the mill settlement where it met its death. Recalling that coyotes had been said to go mad, the man with the injured hand sent the head of the beast to the Pasteur Institute in Portland, received in a day or two the diagnosis of rabies and immediately went down himself for treatment.

"That was the beginning. Coyotes, which are generally very wary, began to appear in barns and dooryards in broad daylight. They fought with the dogs, chased women into the house, and lay down upon the premises till the men of the family came home and shot them. They were killed in the main streets of sizable towns. They came down to feeding grounds where stock is herded for the winter and bit numerous cows and calves in the very presence of the keepers of the herd. Dogs, cows, and calves soon developed hydrophobia. In one district, school was closed out of consideration for the safety of the children.

"A resident of the Basin, a woman who works much in her garden and poultry yard, was one day alarmed by a great uproar in the house, which was supposed to be empty. She called her husband from the field and a rifle happening to be at hand, the two waited outside for what might eventuate. Presently, at an upstairs window, appeared a coyote leaping up and biting at the sash. He was easily shot through the window. He had jumped into a downstairs window and had made his way through the house, leaving marks of his teeth upon the woodwork. In old witch-haunted New England, 'bewitched' wolves did these same daring and unusual things. Thus science is explaining one more superstition.

"Loss of stock and danger to human beings have become so serious that the legislature has been appealed to for a five-dollar bounty on the coyote. This will probably be allowed. The youth of this neighborhood, who would much rather hunt than eat, will presently be lining their pockets with five-dollar-gold pieces—fruit of their hunting and trapping industry. Since the hide of a coyote is worth two or three dollars in itself, the total profit will be considerable. Poor hapless coyote!"

The Journal also contains this snake story:

"Every summer, at just about haying time, rattlesnakes appear in my dooryard. Perhaps they are turned out of the hay fields by the mower. Perhaps in the intense heat of midsummer they are seeking water. Last evening, I was on my way for a pail of water when I heard the familiar warning. Just to the right of the path, under a clump of sage, were two large rattlesnakes. They paid no attention to me after the first signal, but were wholly engrossed with each other. With heads raised perhaps a foot from the ground, they faced each other in some sort of duel—whether friendly or deadly I was unable to determine. They swung to and fro, feinted, recovered, struck, wound their necks together into a cord, extricated themselves, returned to position and repeated the performance. I watched them until I was weary, and, just as I turned away, a smaller and darker rattler ran from the other side of the path and slipped under the two contestants as if for concealment or protection. Were they two gallants contesting for the third—a lady?"

Did I kill them?—the inevitable question. No. "De Lawd give me no mind to."

Just after the snake story, I find so typical an item that, in spite of its irrelevance, I venture to slip it in. It is, at least, not immaterial. "The Nashes called to-day and left me a box of gorgeous new apples and a sheaf of poppies." My book should be illumined with an apple and poppy design, representing the cheer of these good friends who have meant so much to me.

XXIII

THE WITNESS

It was a morning in early May—a day that had arisen early, for the long, long days of our northern summer were rapidly coming on. My pasture slopes were fragrant as a peach orchard with the golden bloom of purshia, and the air was humming with the song of bees. Bossy had failed to make her appearance at the milking hour and I was, not reluctantly, strolling among her favorite hiding places to seek her out. To my surprise I came at length to the outer pasture gate without discovering her, found this gate hanging open, and Bossy's unmistakable track passing through. She had a little nick in the right fore-hoof from some early injury that made her track easy of identification. I recalled now that Psalmmy's clear tenor trumpeting (he was in the adjoining pasture) had waked me at dawn. Here doubtless was the explanation of his uneasiness. It was unusual for Bossy to wander. She was a home-loving creature and, besides, feed was much better in her own pasture than outside.

I followed the track for some little distance in the direction of the highway. Fortunately there had been a rain the night before and the tracks were plain. All at once the tracks were supplemented by those of a horse following and overlying them. I followed both to the highway and for some rods along it. Then I turned about and followed the horse tracks back. The horse had been tied to a juniper at a little distance from the pasture gate and, with some difficulty, I made out a human trail passing under the fence into the pasture. Bossy had been stolen! My wrath, as this conviction forced itself upon me, surprised myself. I was in a blind fury as I raced back for Fly and started in pursuit. For twenty-five miles I followed the tracks without difficulty. The thief had been in haste or he would have avoided the telltale roadway. At the few homes along the route no one had seen the cow and her driver. She had passed in the night. Only at the last house before I reached the village an old man had seen them at dawn.

"Hot she was," he volunteered, "about give out. He'd been drivin' hard." I ground my teeth.

It was not to the village but to an institution in its outskirts that the nicked hoof print led me. Here was an assembly of pens and sheds with fences adorned by numerous hides all comparatively fresh. It was with a chilling apprehension that I ran my eye along the ghastly row in search of a golden tan. It did not appear but, inside the last pen, well supplied with food and drink, recumbent and placid for the moment, with the relief of rest, here was my Bossy. No one was at home in the slaughter house shanty. I dared neither to leave the cow here nor to await the return of the butcher. Indignant and rebellious, Bossy once more took the road and we sought the justice of the peace.

Too plainly the justice was preoccupied. There were larger matters on his slate than this interpolated case of a lost cow. A woman, too—a single woman—always a nuisance—no business to be trying to handle things that belong to a man's province. He put me off irritably. Yes, I might wait, but he was very busy. He rose presently to close the office, and told me grudgingly, neither turning his eyes in my direction nor removing his cigar, that it would be impossible to handle the case to-night. In the morning he would get a jury together. What time? Ten o'clock. Had I witnesses? Could I prove identification? He shook his head disgustedly at my replies. Yes, there was a pound behind the office. He would lock the cow in there. Feed? Certainly not. I might have some brought if I wished. I did. I brought it myself and a pail of water from the livery three blocks away where Fly was stabled.

I found a restaurant and had some supper and a cup of tea which cheered me slightly, but I was very weary and blue. To my vision Bossy was already delivered over to the butcher and led away. I went to bed, but could not sleep. I was trying to hit upon some witness that would be of use. Since Bossy's coming no one but myself had handled her, and a dairy cow in a beef country arouses less than no interest. I doubted whether I had a neighbor who could swear to her identity.

Toward morning I was awakened—electrically awakened—by that same high-pitched trumpeting that had roused me on the previous morning. I was dreaming, of course, but instantly I knew what I should do. I dressed at once and in the gray dawn stole out and sought the telephone. I ate a hearty breakfast and strolled out into the town. Confidence had replaced anxiety. By ten o'clock, however, I was nervous. My witness had not come. Too well I knew for what difficulties and delays that witness might be responsible.

The trial came on promptly. The jury were busy men, none too tolerant of this paltry interruption. "To the butcher with the old cow!" I seemed to hear them saying, "and let us go our ways." I was permitted to tell my tale. The butcher told his. The latter had bought an unbranded cow at a good market price. The owner had received cash payment and had gone his ways. There was a method tested and approved in the stock country for safeguarding live stock. Let him who ignored the custom of the country reap the consequences. An unbranded cow!

The jurymen were with him to a man. I could feel it. Alas, my stock was very low. My lawyer whispered a question. Did the cow know me? Was she friendly? I must have looked blank. The inequalities of Bossy's disposition came heavily to my mind.

"I'll try," I answered. He conferred with the justice. The justice nodded. He gave an order. We would adjourn to the pound. One glance assured me that Bossy was in her blackest mood. She was unmilked and hungry and far from her beloved. As of old, the world was her enemy.

"Bossy"? I appealed quaveringly, approaching on leaden feet. Bossy brandished her imaginary horns at me and retreated. All the moroseness of her earlier days was in her mien.

"Look at that now!" exclaimed the triumphant butcher. "Never seed her before. Don't know her from the man in the moon." I stood literally with hanging head before my condemners. Then something brought us all to attention. A truck had entered the yard behind the high board fence of the pound. And suddenly was heard a clear tenor trumpeting.

"My witness!" I exclaimed jubilantly.

Bossy's sagging muscles snapped into tension and expectancy. Her eyes glowed. She threw up her head and bellowed and started on a run across the yard. Simultaneously, over the high board gate, an apparition! Psalmmy! Light as a bird, ardent as the desert lover! Mother and son rushed together. Meeting in mid-career, they did a waltz or two in the adjustment of their momenta. But Psalmmy's dripping lips had already seized upon one of the swollen teats. A milky slobber already bathed his face. In calflike haste he relieved each teat in turn of its surplus and returned to the attack. His great form rocked and trembled in the fervor of his passion. And Bossy? Her dreamy eyes gazing heavenward, she was already chewing the cud of sublime content.

The bored jury had come to attention with the very first exchange of greeting between mother and son. Stockmen, every one of them, they felt something was in the air. Amazement superseded expectancy. A ripple of amusement followed that. Psalmmy, half-way through his meal, became conscious of spectators. He withdrew his lips from the font and turned his great countenance upon the jury, imbued with all the meek and milky innocence of a new-born calf. Amusement became mirth and mirth hilarity. Laughter shook the little group like a summer breeze. They clapped one another upon the shoulder and roared. They smote their thighs and bent double in the ecstasy of their glee. They leaned against the fence and its foundations quivered. My lawyer appeared to be hugging each of the jurors in turn. The justice collapsed upon a hydrant. The butcher alone maintained his dignity and viewed the scene with glum disfavor.

"Look a-here," he protested, "how do you know it's *her* steer?" indicating me.

My lawyer looked a question. I nodded.

Psalmmy, meanwhile, who always took less than a fourth of the time for his milking that I did, had finished his repast and was exchangiing with Bossy the courtesies of the morning toilet—the cow-licks that adorn the silky coats of the well-beloved. I approached—this time with confidence. "Psalmmy," I called. Psalmmy turned about at once. He identified me at a glance. Deliberately he braced his feet. His back came up into a bow. He drew in his chin and arched his neck. His whole frame trembled as, with a mighty effort, he brought from the depths of his being a long-drawn "b-a-a-a-w!"

A renewed tempest of laughter passed over the group behind me. Not a man among them but was familiar with this greeting of the friendly "bos."

But I had done with them. My hand was in the velvet folds of Psalmmy's neck and my cheek against his. We heard the juniper birds calling from the pasture and smelled the fragrance of the purshia.

XXIV

PLOWING

AUTUMN of this fourth year brought me a new and large experience. Putting in my own field crop was the one activity of the farm that I had not essayed. I had thought it beyond me. Once more, however, I was left in the lurch. My contractor, who had engaged early and with all due formality, escaped to Canada. I saw ruin staring me in the face, for every lost crop meant a season's buying of feed for the chickens and for my little "bunch" of stock. A friend had left a well-broken horse with me for the season, in order that I might have a mate for Fly. Thus it was by the way of much tribulation that I advanced at last to the acquisition of a team of my own, to the loan of a walking plow, and to faith in my own ability to plow and seed my own sweet acres.

Before three acres had been overturned I had demonstrated several truths beyond dispute, viz., that, having acquired team and plow, there yet remain to the novice amazing difficulties in the assembling of the same; that that small and modest bow of iron known as the clevis is of importance inestimable in the economy of the field; that the graduate in the manipulation of bolts and levers, to the end that the furrow may be just deep enough and the plow may turn just "land" enough, is a sadder and a wiser being; that it matters essentially whether, in the circumlocution of the field, the field be had upon the right or left; that the natural position of the walking plow is on its side and that it exercises admirable persistency in retiring to that position at every opportunity; that there is a divinity that shapes the end of a furrow and also various demons—judging from the shapes personally achieved; that one's team, however faithful, shares the universal preference for the line of least resistance and discovers in the course of a few rounds that it eases the strain materially for the furrow horse to depart from the furrow; that the excruciating "bot fly" has a traditional understanding of the helplessness of a plow team to flee from him and improves his opportunities accordingly, an understanding shared by the ever-present colt, who acts upon this intelligence by running in between the plow horses and depositing with them his own pursuing tormentor; that beneath the surface of the innocent soil lurk snares and dangers manifold—stumps whose eradication had been duly paid for, snags capable of parting horse and whiffletree and of rending whiffletrees asunder; that a horse may step over his trace as many times in a morning as there are angles in his course, and, to sum up all, that the "plowboy's weary way" is more truly fact than poetry.

Three acres had been overturned, presenting a varied scene as to depth, symmetry of lines, and width of furrow. Thirty-seven acres stretched ahead—seemingly, though the unspeakably weary plowman dared not admit it to herself, an insurmountable task. Then Mary De Long, one of those practical friends who make the world go 'round, lightly and casually suggested the loan of a riding plow and an extra horse. It is deeds like this that are remembered in heaven.

Unquestionably we have an hereditary craving and instinct for the touch of the soil. There is a peculiar depth of satisfaction in rolling it up before the plowshare and in combing it to a powdered fineness. Before the magic of my riding plow previous difficulties smoothed themselves out, like troubled waters before the touch of the god. My own team, taking their cue from the faultless furrow horse who was our guest, bent their heads to patient and obedient plodding on the endless round. I was as happy, perched on my little iron seat, training my acres to productive usefulness, as the air man, the ship master, or the autoist. Day by day my triple team became my closer and more understanding friends. I felt a more and more tender appreciation of their patient strength, their docility in weariness, their gentle acceptance of their toilsome fate, their confidence in my provision of the abundant ration in the enjoyment of which they sank all sorrows, all regrets.

I learned that it is well to establish quite strictly a schedule of work and hold to it, not only for its showing in the steady accumulation of results but because one's horses are accurate timekeepers—cheerful within the schedule, but brokenhearted at the imposition of over time. Each day I knew by their quickened step and eager ears when we had reached the last round before noon, and that when we should have won to the shade of a certain juniper the point of its shadow would fall toward Pilot Butte, our northern pole. How confidently they halted there, tossing their heads and looking around at me! I loved to slip off each piece of heavy harness and give them, one by one, their freedom and to see them gallop off across the field—pausing perhaps for a luxurious roll in the new-turned earth—to the certainty of drink and dinner.

"To-morrow and to-morrow and to-morrow!" Concentric square within concentric square, dawn and the plow, nooning and the plow, night. All else on the farm stood still that the plowing might go forward. And when at last we had turned under that central clod, upon which our eyes had rested for so many days, it was only to enter upon the long period of harrowing and seeding. It was not convenient to get a seeder, hence I sowed my seed like the patriarchs—straight from the shoulder. Day after day I walked and scattered thinking often of kindergarten training days when I had lightly sung and gestured: "Shall we show you how the farmer, Shall we show you how the farmer, Shall we show you how the farmer sows his wheat in the spring?" Just a trifle bitterly perhaps I recalled the lightness, with a touch of the laborer's resentment, when aching arms almost refused to move and knees cracked with excessive exercise. And, alternately with the sowing, was the folding in—the last smoothing of the harrow, the last lap of the journey. Ready for rain and sun now, for heat and cold, for frost and thaw. Human solicitude can do no more.

And the spiritual fruits of the plowing? Rare leisure and opportunity to observe the sky, the shifting sun, the maturing season; rare chance to cultivate the confidence of the little birds that find treasure trove in the upturned soil and learn merely to hop to right or left and to answer our hail with cheerful chirpings; rare chance to pity the poor evicted creatures of the soil—dazed and paralyzed little mice and moles turned from their dark catacombs into the blazing day, mighty Babylons of red ants upon whom their city "is fallen, is fallen."

"Oh, Life! Oh, Life—sad and tragic, unbelievably cruel, pitiful and hopeless, glad, triumphant, blithe, and gay!"

Plowing

HERITAGE

"Ancestral acres," who falls heir
Thereto in ghostly company
Of prince and lord and feudal chief—
Who held dominion harsh and brief
And drew their selfish barriers close
'Twixt mead and spring and haunted wood
And trespass of the common hind —
In fellowship of such he tills
Neglected and depleted fields
And for the sport of such preserves
The gracious life the forest yields.

Who breaks a homestead in the West
And leads the trickling water through
Where all was parched and brown and bare—
Converts a plain of stark distress
To green delights and loveliness—
Who makes a lean land bountiful
For man and beast and winged bird,
With him his great Creator walks,
In kinship on his faithful round;
And with him Gardener Adam talks
The language of ancestral ground.

XXV

THE OLD OREGONIAN AGAIN

A NEW teacher had been installed in the district schoolhouse. I had not had the opportunity of meeting her but, from certain infallible proofs, I had gathered that she was no bromide. In fact, I more than suspected that dangerous fires were in process of generation, and I wished that I might be of some moral support to her. I stopped one afternoon as I came from the post office.

The young teacher received me with a veiled defensiveness that I thought I understood, and took pains to dispel.

The class were drawing the district map—fitting in ranch-houses, roads, and creeks, and noting in the corners crops raised, native herbs, grains, and trees. The work showed careful observation and much pains. I became enthusiastic. The teacher warmed to me and explained that she had been conducting excursions in the interest of geography, agriculture, drawing, etc., and that there had been much criticism in consequence. The board were to meet with her that afternoon to consult about it. The board presently appeared, and the school was dismissed. I was about to go, but caught an appeal in the eye of the defendant and sat down at once.

The Old Oregonian was in the chair. I was glad to see that, in the presence of the dignified young pedagoguess, and under the influence of the recent unmistakable and graceful attentions to the battered old schoolroom, it was with some difficulty that he brought forward the complaints that had been lodged with him. It appeared, he said, that the pupils had been wasting time idling about out of doors when they should have been in the schoolroom. There had even been some irregularity of hours and program (the unpardonable sin). One pupil had lost a book in one of the jaunts referred to. Then they had been required to do work that was not fitting. They had been asked to dust, scrub, and decorate the schoolroom, to make curtains, and had even built a shed for their horses—the horses which had stood out in the blizzards for twenty-five years—and all this in time that should have been devoted to books. The Old Oregonian gradually warmed to his theme. The district employed a teacher to teach book-learning, he said, and, if she couldn't do that, it was best that they should know it.

It came time at last for the accused to state her case. She did it well. She was a little pale, but, with sincere and patient effort, she sought to explain the aims and methods of the newer education.

The chairman and his colleagues chewed, and spat upon the newly-whitened floor, and waited with an air of suspended animation till their turn should come again. At length, the Old Oregonian held up a restraining hand.

"Naow, naow," he protested. "That may all do where you come from, but it won't do here, an' it ain't what we pay for. Why, we've run school in this district for twenty-five year, an' we ain't never had this sort o' goin's on, an' we don't want it neither. We ain't got nothing against you, Miss Hawley, but we know what we want you to learn them pupils, an' we're goin' to have it done. Now the program what's been followed in this district for twenty-five year is in that register yonder, an' we'd like for you to stick to that an' make the pupils learn."

I had been busy with the State Course of Study. In a pause, I rose with apologies and showed how the new teacher's work was in line with the prescribed course, and had the sanction of the Superintendent.

Again that restraining hand. "That may all be so, Miss Andromeda, but we ain't never done that way here. Them may be the ways o' them high-toned folks at the capital, but they ain't our ways. Now my instructions is," he concluded, "to ask this young lady to do our way or to let us know."

He fixed his cool, gray eyes upon the victim with

unmistakable finality, adjourned the meeting, and went out to his waiting horse.

A few days later, as I passed the schoolhouse, Miss Hawley called me in. She was putting finishing touches to the room, and preparing to depart. She had resigned.

"It's not temper," she explained. "It's not obstinacy, please believe me. "It's professional honor. The sooner our laws and customs give us teachers the rights and privileges of specialists the better it'll be for education, and it's my conviction that some of us must make a stand. Imagine sending expert engineers to the tropics, and requiring them to educate the natives to an appreciation of up-to-date engineering before they dig a canal or build a bridge. That's what they're asking of us."

At the post office, I encountered the Old Oregonian. "Jane Slade kin finish out the term," he was saying. "She ain't very bright, but she's raised here an' knows what we want. I reckon she'll do."

But it remained for Sunday school to set the stage for personal combat between the Old Oregonian and myself. All the way down from the Creation to the Exodus, the Old Oregonian and I had spatted and sparred. I had acted upon the conviction that a neighborhood religious gathering should be an open court for interchange of serious opinion. In all sincerity and apropos of the story of Creation, I had presented the known truths of Evolution with the enthusiasm of the amateur scientist. Two Sabbaths proved adequate for branding me as "The *In*-fi-*dell!*"

My unwillingness to credit the Supreme Mind with the cruel and illogical "plan of salvation," the roots of which were (traditionally) laid in this early period of the world's history, aroused inimical emotions in the breasts of the Old Oregonian and his friends. That the Eden story might partake of the nature of allegory, that the Hebrew's belief in his own exclusive enjoyment of the favor of the Almighty might be but a partial and human view, that the Lord might have been less tricky in his dealings with Pharaoh than the biblical account implies—such suggestions met abrupt and unqualified opposition.

"Naow, naow"—the Old Oregonian rises to the occasion. "If we ain't able to study Scriptur an' let alone findin' fault with it, maybe we'd best stay home an' pray for grace. Ain't we been comin' to this here schoolhouse off an' on for thirty year an' ain't found it necessary to hold opinions outside o' what's regular an' orthodox?"

"Open the eyes o' the blind, O Lord," he prayed each Sunday. "Snatch thy brands from the burning."

As a rule, the questions assigned to me from the printed questionnaire in the quarterly were carefully selected. Inadvertently, however, it fell to me one

Sunday to give a summing up of the character of Jacob.

"Judged by our highest standards of conduct," I said, "he was a precious rascal of an old Jew."

Then did the Old Oregonian rise in his wrath, and over events immediately sequential I draw the veil.

"Why, the old fellow's been conducting his cattle deals on the Jacobean style 'for thirty year,' " explained the lawyer son of one of my neighbors. "You knocked out his main prop."

XXVI

TO HAVE AND TO HOLD

THE term of residence required for proving up on my original filing was now fulfilled, but, unfortunately, some mythical citizen had filed, at some time long past, upon my desired additional—filed and utterly disappeared. A term of advertising was therefore necessary in order to give him time to assert his rights if he so desired. Thus another winter slipped by without special incident. It contained hardships and growing debts. Feed was all to be bought. The diligence of my hens and Bossy's irreproachable milk and cream could not compensate for my repeated crop failures "before the fact." They did, however, remove all danger of my going hungry, and Fly's strong willingness assured my supply of fuel and my easy communication with the outside world.

A Journal note of earlier date suggests of how large concern was another change that this season brought about.

"If I have loved truly any creature—beast or human—I have truly loved my dogs. If I have received from any true affection, I have received it from my dogs. They rise before me—a wistful line of those that have claimed my heart—little white mongrel with speaking eyes, golden collie, glossy black Newfoundlands, many a pathetic wayfarer whom circumstances or stern relatives removed from the sphere of my attentions, and, last and present forever at my feet or under my hand's caress, or racing hither and yon, in conjunction with my various jaunts, Bingo—Bingo, already of a decade's inseparable companionship, Bingo of the shaggy, red-brown coat, the ebullient physical vivacity and joy of living, the passionate, unswerving devotion."

It was during this winter that the shadow of age began to fall upon my inseparable companion. I remember the day when, to my amazement, he wagged farewell to Fly and me and lay patiently down upon the porch to await our return. He had ceased to compete with her upon the road. For a time, he still showed delight in the prospect of a walk to the mail box, but gradually even this became more than his measure. From shadowing me about the place on my many excursions, he grew to content himself with taking up his position where he could keep an eye upon me, rising always when I returned to the house to slip his moist nose into my hand and wag his eloquent tail in apology for failing attentions. At times he would brighten up, assume a puppyish demeanor and coax me to throw sticks for him to retrieve, in our old fashion of playing. Gradually lethargy grew upon him, and, like an old man, his wants became confined to a warm corner, food and drink, and the near presence of one whom he loved.

It was fitting that my lone-hand crop should be final witness to the good faith and sincerity of my homesteading—my proving-up crop. It was a beautiful one—the season being exceptionally fine—and I loved it in its developing phases, as an artist loves the landscapes of his own creation. I had not planned to "play it alone" at harvesting as well as seeding time, but fate would have it so. It had been a peculiarly lonely year for me. My particular friends among the homesteaders, whose term of residence a little antedated mine, had already proved up and several had sought other fields for the reimbursing of their depleted fortunes. Crops were large that year and help an almost unknown quantity.

So it was that, as yellow began to tinge the fields, desperate with the fear of losing what had cost so much, I set to work with a scythe and, working at night in order to avoid the heat of the day—the moon being at the full—I had actually cut about two acres, when a human-hearted rancher bethought him of an old mower that was idle. This was put in repair for me, Fly and her companion bent their willing necks to the task, and my heavy waves of grain bowed obediently before the circling mower, illustrating, as had the riding plow in the fall, the superiority of the age of invention. I still had no plan for the raking. It seemed that every hayrake in the countryside was overworked. Once more I set to work by hand, but this time my friends the Nashes stepped into the breach. A hayrake was forthcoming and the day was saved. Could I stack it alone? I confess it looked impossible. I could do no less than begin, however, and begin I did. For one month, "through long days of labor and nights devoid of ease," I tossed and stacked one hundred thousand pounds of hay—twenty-five tons lifted twice—suspending every other activity save milking and chicken feeding, living on boiled eggs, crackers, and milk, while I tossed and tossed and stacked from morn till dewy eve. Nor was I in the end one whit the worse for the experience. When the last load was on the last stack and I realized that I had made a crop from the hauling of the seed to the last folding away of the last straw, I sat down beneath the haystack, while Fly and her mate nibbled unchecked at the heads of wheat, and gave to the world the inspired version that had been turning itself in my head the while I tossed:

The Making of the Hay

By Friar Butte's rugged hill slopes,
Out Crooked River way,
By junipers surrounded,
There stand three stacks of hay.

And no man stirred the fallow fields
And no man touched the hay,
For a lone old maid that hay crop made
And packed the stuff away.

That was the fairest harvest
That ever turned to gold.
That was the gladdest mowing
Since ages hoar and old.
And never winds of morning
From Nature's fragrant plain
Did lightlier pass o'er virgin grass
Than o'er that rippling grain.

And was it not high honor
To turn the pristine sod,
To lightly fold the seeds away
And leave the rest to God?
As in the infant ages,
So grew through cold and heat
The ancient feast of man and beast—
The immemorial wheat!

This summer of nineteen-sixteen, I was already overdue on the other side of the continent for an extended visit. I had not quite shaken off the bonds of old association, and the ties of blood were calling me. A teaching position awaited me there for the term of my visit, and I looked to straighten out the kinks in my homestead finances before I should return again to the bucolic life. My departure awaited only the last act in the drama—the making of final proof of requisite residence and improvement.

To Have and to Hold

It was a strangely significant day to me when I rode Fly to town for the last time. No brown shadow whisked and exulted beside us and my ride was saddened by the thought of the drooping of that friend who for thirteen years had shared my every experience. It was only a brief ceremony—the business at the land office. My proof was incontestable, my witnesses were on hand—the Nashes and the DeLongs—and I had ample time to arrange for my ticket east and to see the friendly dairyman who was to care for Bossy and Psalmmy, Fly and Babe. The white flock was also placed with a farmer on the edge of town, and I made part of the trip back to Broadview on that same evening.

It was like a stroke of fate that only five days before my intended departure, old Bingo failed for the first time to get upon his feet in the morning. He was partially paralyzed. For a day or two I carried him in and out, but he was in pain and had reached the point where only a final sleep could ease him. I had long had the fatal dose of morphine on hand, looking toward this necessity and now I administered it, he accepting it obediently and hopefully, as I felt, remembering other doses that had given him relief. He licked up a drop or two that had been spilled upon the floor and very quickly grew quiet and fell asleep. The pain he had been suffering followed him into his dreams and caused him to moan. I placed my hand upon his head and instantly the moaning ceased and sleep came upon him that knew no waking.

Came the last evening at Broadview. How very still it was! No softly-cropping creatures stealing about in the twilight. No snowy chanticleer—popping his head out suddenly to challenge the rising moon. No warm and heavy head upon my knee. I was very glad and cheerful, I thought, in the prospect of my home-going. I was satisfied with all my arrangements for Broadview and its one-time tenants, yet all unheeded, in my absorption with thoughts of past and present, tears were raining down my face. The sense of the closing of a chapter was upon me, the rending of that little circle brute and human that had drawn itself close and closer about this rare, bright chapter of my life. "It takes something from the heart and it never comes again."

Some months later, as I sat at breakfast in an eastern city, a long envelope bearing the seal of the Department of the Interior was delivered to me. From this envelope I drew forth a document bearing in turn the seal of the United States of America. It was my patent and it declared that my claim to "the southeast quarter and the south half of the northeast quarter and the lot one, Section Four, Township Seventeen, Range Nineteen East, Willamette Meridian—being three hundred and nineteen and seventy one-hundredths acres"—had been duly consummated, that it was mine "to have and to hold," to be the lawful right of my "heirs and assigns forever." "In testimony whereof, I, WOODROW WILSON, President of the United States, have caused these letters to be made patent and the seal of the General Land Office to be affixed."

XXVII

AFTERWORD

IN this year of our Lord nineteen hundred and twenty-one, ten years since that Thanksgiving Day of glorious hopes, I still cling to the homestead dream. I have known lean years and leaner years, hope and discouragement, good fortune and disaster, friendship and malice, righteousness, generosity, and double dealing.

My difficulties have been far oftener with the human element than with the rigors of the climate or the hardships of labor. The most melancholy theme of my homestead experience, and one that I approach only with trepidation and misgiving, is the management of men. I began this chapter of my life with certain hypotheses, even convictions, somewhat as follows: Men are innately chivalrous, men will respond in kind to frank and just dealing, men will appreciate trust and confidence and will justify the same. I continue the chapter with a number of open questions which may be stated as follows: Is real chivalry the flower alone of the highest culture and the utmost refinement? Is that which masks as chivalry lower down merely a sex phenomenon—a means to a purely selfish end? Is straight dealing between man and man often a concession to fear—merely a politic observance, the benefits of which a woman may not share? What proportion of our citizenry regard a promise, the fulfillment of which entails some loss or inconvenience to the promiser, as better broken than kept? Does the easy promiser continue to believe in his own promises or is he perfidious in the very making of them? Can one rely upon any real respect for justice in the so-called lower order of men, or do these act universally upon self-interest and prejudice?

During my two years' absence in the East, the care of Broadview having been carefully and legally arranged for, my neighbors' cattle fattened upon my growing crops and exploited my excellent pasture, ruining it for years to come. My fences, the care of which was to have been my only compensation for the full use of the pasture, were flat upon the ground and stock roamed at will throughout the place. Since my return, I have had a valuable Jersey calf mutilated, and Bossy—mother of all my little herd—ruthlessly killed for straying into a neighbor's pasture over *his* down fence.

Ah, well! I have said I still cling to the dream. Now and then I have known burdens—most often physical burdens—too heavy for mortals to bear. I have been cold and hungry and ragged and penniless. I have been free and strong and buoyant and glad. Over my six hundred and forty acres—thus increased by a second beneficent allowance—roams a beautiful little Jersey herd. A group of dear white ponies call me mistress. White biddies still dot my hill slopes and cackle ceaselessly. Pax, an Armistice Day puppy, and El Dorado, son of Kitty Kat, have succeeded those earlier friends whose gentle spirits still wander with me on the sagebrush slopes. There is a mortgage. There is still necessity to teach. My little flock of orphan citizens still beckon from the future. Yet, for me, the wilderness and the solitary place have been glad, and Nature has not betrayed the heart that loved her.

A Tribute

To those who, in the pilgrims' land,
Have moved my life to happy ends
And, through the seasons' wearing round,
Have earned the sacred name of friends;

To those with whom at household board
Or in the forest's festal shade
I've broken bread and drained the cup
And silent vows of fealty made;

For trust in one who, far from home,
Nor fame nor champion could boast,
For gentle deeds of kindness done
The stranger on the foreign coast;

Afterword

For quick'ning word, for helpful hand,
  For unsaid thought and kindling glance,
For generous plan, for happy jaunt,
  And many a joy-filled circumstance—

To these, for such, through all the years
  My love is warm for evermore,
For these my tepee's sheltering walls
  Hold hospitality in store.

8087